The Compression Planning Advantage: Exploding the Meeting Myth

First Edition

Jerry McNellis
Assisted by:
Jack Nettles &
Pat McNellis

Does the slow pace of decision making in your organization frustrate you?

Does your organization have projects and issues that never seem to get resolved, projects that seldom get completed on time, or strategies that languish?

Available at:
CompressionPlanning.com &
Amazon.com

10.25.2021

M-22013   10.21   B2291

'What People Say About Compression Planning'

"I was 28 years old (it was 1983) and asked to put together a group of experts from electric utilities to develop a national R&D plan. We hired Jerry to train our facilitators and I have been using his techniques ever since to run small, medium, and large meetings.

I believe Jerry's teaching and concepts have not just helped me in planning meetings but also in critical and strategic thinking. People are always amazed at how much we can get done in large groups with effective planning and facilitation."

Jonathan W. Hurwitch
Executive Vice President
Sentech, Inc.
Bethesda, MD

"Efficiency is what we were seeking; consensus is what we got as a byproduct. This is a very focused way of getting people on board.

The Board really liked it. Comments like 'this is exactly what we needed' were the rule vs. the exception.

Take any task – eliminate the what we are not here to address – outline what we need to do – get at the 'to do's' and get everyone to literally sign on for their role.

We have a construction project and a capital campaign - this process is very useful for both. We used the process for our Board retreat – the Board really liked it.

Focus – keep everyone on task.

You won't find a better group of people with whom to work and their experience makes the process extremely efficient and cost effective. It will save you a lot of meetings."

Raymond B. White
Chief Executive Officer
The Watson Institute
Sewickley, PA

"I first learned about Compression Planning in the early 1980s and have been using it since. We recently trained 18 colleagues to use Compression Planning and they are using it in a variety of ways. We've had sessions that clarified the organization of details for our new international campus, planned a move into a new building complete with thousands of details on a very short timeline, and prioritized daily activities."

Tom Botzman, Ph.D.
VP Business & Finance
St. Mary's College of Maryland
St. Mary's City, MD

"Every time I've used Compression Planning, it's been a huge time-saver for the participants. I'd say absolutely 75% savings in time."

Jay Duffy
Retired Dir., Executive Development and Leadership
Bayer Corporation
Pittsburgh, PA

"My purpose for learning the Compression Planning process was simple: an agency (National Institute of Corrections) who contracts with me uses the Compression Planning process on a fairly routine basis.

I was thrilled as I'd been impressed by how quickly NIC staff...utilizing the Compression Planning process...were able to develop very complete plans to solve fairly complex problems in very short periods of time.

The Compression Planning training is masterfully designed. Participants bring real-world projects and apply the Compression Planning process to those ideas, projects etc. The ability to take a goal (in some cases a thought) to a sold plan in a matter of a few hours and have truly great minds (the other participants) from a broad variety of back grounds help with the planning – what a deal!

This system has been one of the most valuable tools in my tool chest."

Winnie Ore
President, Western Training and Consulting
'Center of the Enhancement of Human Potential' LLC
Helena, MT

'What People Say About Compression Planning'

"Compression Planning really levels the playing field, and one of the things people like best about the process is it's fun! Many, many times I hear 'This is the best planning session I've ever been in.' It spans the gap for everyone. If you're no-nonsense, you'll like it for that reason. If you're creative, you'll like it because it allows you to be very creative and open to a lot of different directions."

Peter R. Hughes
Market Vice President - Business Development
Advocate Christ Medical Center
Advocate Hope Children's Hospital
Advocate Trinity Hospital
Oak Lawn, IL

"Most recently, we had the opportunity to use Compression planning in one of the LLC's that has a total of four partners. One of the partners is the managing partner and is at the business every day. The other three of us are there one day a month for guidance and consultation.

We needed the best way to herd cats. Each of the four partners are entrepreneurs and we needed to act collaboratively. We needed to get together to put a strategic plan together for 2008, and we only had one day to do it. Some parts of the plan are to increase sales by 20% (measurable) and improve throughput by 30% (measurable), and do it at the same cost.

The plan was put together in one day, with a planned one-day follow-up with two additional people to lay out some specific detail on equipment moves."

Bob McDemus
Partner, Reneuxit LLC
Westchester, PA

"I had seen first-hand many Compression Planning techniques used by a new supervisor who arrived at the College soon after my arrival. I was so impressed that when the College offered the opportunity to participate in the McNellis Compression Planning Institute I altered my vacation plans to attend.

I was certainly not disappointed and learned more than I had ever hoped toward getting to the root of an issue and arriving at a solution in a more effective and efficient manner."

George W. Waggoner
Director, Campus Technology Support Services
St. Mary's College of Maryland
St. Mary's City, MD

"I took the class back in the fall of 1988. I still have the binder and still refer to it. It was probably the most useful seminar in my career...stuff I could apply immediately.

The Compression Planning techniques I learned are key elements in starting our major projects. I see two big benefits of the techniques. One is the ability to compress the time it takes to get started. Without Compression Planning, we could probably collect all that stuff in other ways but it would take longer – in some cases, a lot longer. In other cases, it might be impossible.

The second benefit is that Compression Planning helps us reach consensus as a group. It's essential to get our clients in agreement and in some kind of alignment. The technique does that because all the decisions the group makes are visible and they're irrefutable. When we have agreement, we can move a project forward."

Don Moyer
Co-Founder, ThoughtForm Inc. - Information Architects
Pittsburgh PA
Among their many prestigious clients are Hamburger University at McDonald's, Steelcase, Caterpillar, BearingPoint, and Otis.

'What People Say About Compression Planning'

"I used Compression Planning through-out our Lean Six Sigma implementation at Dormont Manufacturing Company.

A key to success for any Six Sigma team is creativity and getting the input of all the resources on the team. Speed also helps the process to not falter and keeps team meetings productive. These are all hallmarks of Compression Planning. It was always my contention that every Black Belt (leaders of Lean Six Sigma Projects) should be a trained and experienced Compression Planning facilitator."

Michael A. Couch
President
Michael Couch & Associates Inc.
Pittsburgh, PA

"I've experienced the effectiveness of Compression Planning many times. It enables people to work in a much more efficient and effective manner and allows them to pursue more opportunities.

I know the investment in the training will be returned tenfold."

Pat Gerity Ph.D.
VP Cont. Ed/ Workforce & Community Dev.
Westmoreland County Community College
Youngwood, PA

"CP is at the base of everything I do. It's kind of like Lamaze. I got into it for one reason and then found applications for it in so many other aspects of my life. Sometimes faculty members have an idea of what they want to do and they're not really sure how to make it specific. How do they make it into a form that we can apply for a grant and fund their idea?

For example, one group I did Compression Planning with involved four cooperating organizations who wanted to help girls get more interested in science. We received a four-year grant for $800,000."

Pamela Jira
Executive Dir. Foundation/Assistant to the President
Zane State College
Zanesville, OH

"We've found CP really helpful in providing direction and priorities for the grants we apply for a yearly planning period. It helps get all the entities and departments on board for what we are going to do...the priorities...they buy in to the collective agenda and where we'll spend our efforts.

The biggest benefit for us has been to get people on the same page priority-wise. When you work in higher education, people have their own agendas with their own priorities. Compression Planning helps people see and appreciate the big picture in the mission of the larger university."

Chris Shaw
Grants and Projects Coordinator
Ohio University
Zanesville, OH

"I used CP to help teams of employees coming together from three different nuclear plants to develop common processes that would be implemented as the standard across our fleet. We worked on establishing common processes for everything from the procedures we use to perform work to how we make design modifications to nuclear power plants.

Besides being an effective tool, CP really did make a very difficult job a little easier for the folks involved. These employees were asked to develop these common processes in addition to their normal work so they were only able to come together periodically.

For these teams, CP was a life saver."

Jeanny Amidon
...in her work with First Energy
Toledo, OH

'What People Say About Compression Planning'

"We were approached by a school district to write a grant. It was really complex because it involved three federal agencies and a host of community partners. Doing a grant with one department of the federal government is tough enough. Working with three federal departments is unbelievably complex – and we only had two weeks to pull it all together and submit it.

The competition for the grant was fierce and people all over the country were applying for it. Their people had done lots of the background work that needed to be pulled together and focused. Everyone thought there wasn't a chance to get the grant; however, we took it on.

In two meetings...one for about two hours...another for one hour...we used Compression Planning and identified all the parts and pieces and most importantly, identified the holes...the gaps that were missing and assigned them to people to be completed.

I know without Compression Planning that school district and their partners would not have been awarded the $9 million grant."

John Jeanetta
Vice President of Organizational Development
AIM Institute
Omaha, NE

"Recently, the Boston Consulting Group released a study showing that 80% of CEOs think that innovation is critical to their future, but less than half of them think they are doing a good job with it. It also showed that we have lots and lots of good ideas, but were not commercializing them. To me that means there are probably one of two things happening. Either the good ideas aren't good enough to capture the imagination and passion of the people OR, they don't have a process in place to successfully implement ideas.

Compression Planning does both of those things. It can take a good idea and make it great...and it creates an environment that allows passion and engagement to emerge, which greatly enhances the likelihood of successful implementation."

Joyce Wycoff
Founder, InnovationNetwork
Bakersfield, CA

"Compression Planning is the core methodology in my consulting practice. It is what I am getting to be known for as a business consultant. I use it in one way or another in each and every one of my work engagements.

Use it with your family, with your church, at your work, in your personal decisions. Use it and you will find it to be a great tool to add to your life skills."

Alfredo Enrique Umaña
Director, Applied Consulting
Tegucigalpa, Honduras
Central America

"When you need quick decisions, when you're bringing a lot of diverse people to the table with different agendas and different motivations, Compression Planning keeps everyone focused on the target goals."

Mary Jo D'Orazio
Manager, Training and Organization Development
Services, Human Resources
Denver International Airport,
Denver, CO

"The Compression Planning System is by far the single-most effective tool I have learned in all of my travels through two masters degrees and a gazillion workshops."

Jan Nedin
Performance Solutions Architect
Five Star Development, Inc.
Pittsburgh, PA

"Frankly, I went to my first CP workshop as something of a skeptic. Many times, such workshops have provided interesting information and a chance to meet good people, but rarely do they live up to their billing.

In any case, I attended because I recognized that my work depended on the ability to get productive and timely work from groups. At the time, our state department of education had just mandated the development of comprehensive district plans in just about every area related to teaching and learning; each had a requirement for a quick turnaround and each one required that

'What People Say About Compression Planning'

the product—the plan—be the result of collaboration among faculty, administrators and parents.

I was looking for insights into group process and group dynamics—a few useful hints, perhaps. What I got was a very different way of looking at things, one that focused on results yet still provided those involved with the respect, dignity and opportunities for meaningful input they deserved. After completing the training, I was able to go back to my school district, work with diverse groups to develop the required plans, and include in those plans really meaningful goals, activities and program assessments.

I've been a proponent since then—and I've used it in countless ways: strategic planning, program design, program assessment, personnel evaluation, presentations to the community, and team building."

Robert Feirsen, Ed.D.
Superintendent
Garden City Public Schools
Garden City, NY

"Our work teams find this remarkable system has documented bottom-line results:
- Time to completion drops an estimated 50%
- Errors and mistakes drop an estimated 40%

Most importantly, a sense of total ownership for the process grows among employees '10 fold.' What makes this system particularly unique in today's over tech world is that it does this without the use of a computer, without any costly hardware.

What used to take us weeks now takes hours with the 'thinking technology' that drives the Compression Planning system."

Doug Hall
Founder and CEO of the world famous Eureka! Ranch
Newtown, OH
...uses the system to plan every inventing project he conducts for his impressive client list:
Nike, Walt Disney, Ford Motor Company, American Express, Hewlett Packard

"Jerry not only helped me to create a relationship with a group of people I had no experience with, but also turned that session into a results-oriented meeting that will generate benefits for some time to come. He did an excellent job of staying on task to make sure we accomplished what I had intended from this session and then generated a document that helped us follow-up in the weeks and months ahead. Thanks Jerry!!"

Scott Schrank
Vice President, Hampton Brand Management
Hilton Hotels Corporation
Memphis, TN

"I worked for a large public relations agency that was asked to constantly write proposals, which took a lot of thinking and agency time to develop. Some clients would hire us, but a lot of people would simply steal our ideas and recommendations.

Compression Planning helped us solve this problem, not as a brainstorming means for ourselves but as a product we would offer clients. We sold it as the 'first step' in working with a client. We used it to explore their current situation, brainstorm possible solutions and prioritize a set of recommendations.

Compression Planning solved two problems. First, it allowed us to get paid for writing a proposal (about $5,000 for a two-hour session with two to three agency and two to three client representatives). Second, our proposal acceptance went way up, because we were now giving recommendations and we already had a chance to start proving ourselves in the kick-off meeting.

Since that time, I've used CP frequently for strategic planning, developing marketing plans and other consensus-building activities. It continues to work great and continues to turn unpaid meetings into events that clients love and that produce results."

Lloyd Corder, Ph.D.
President & CEO
CorCom, Inc.
Pittsburgh, PA

'What People Say About Compression Planning'

"The project was for the Air Force because they wanted to determine whether Saddam Hussein was detonating any nuclear devices.

Six of us did a Compression Planning session – a machine shop supervisor, two machinists, one sheet metal mechanic, Dr. Shell and I. As a young scientist, Dr. Shell was involved with the Manhattan Project that built the first atomic bomb.

We storyboarded for about two-thirds of a day and planned the whole thing! When we went out of there, we knew exactly what we wanted. We knew what specific pieces of instrumentation we needed. We knew how we had to have everything mounted. We had everything we needed to start construction.

The Air Force was able to take air samples and feed it through our device to tell whether any nuclear gases, as a result of nuclear fission, were released into the atmosphere. The air samples could be taken from 1,000 miles away from the site they wanted to check."

Don Bolland
Owner, Bolland Machine
Chippewa Township, PA

"I was looking for something that was new and unique to planning. I needed something that was different than writing on flip charts where we had no way to organize or develop an action plan.

Part of my job with the Bureau of Prisons as the Distance Learning Administrator is to produce all Satellite-Internet Broadcasts, where we produce all types of training and I use Compression Planning to plan the programs.

There are so many ways that this can be used. I am pushing to convince my administration to use this method with all the unnecessary meetings that we must sit through.

You could use this method to plan a multibillion dollar project to a small project."

Edward C Wolahan
Correctional Program Specialist
Dept. of Justice, National Institute of Corrections
Aurora, CO

"Jerry McNellis and Compression Planning allowed us to develop a team and transition our small company from a crisis-driven managed organization to a proactive, growing international company. Using Jerry's techniques, we opened up communications across all lines of the company and destroyed those 'silos' that get in the way of being great.

Compression Planning not only gets your team excited to change, but forces you to execute that change. We are a small food company with great products in a niche business. We were structured to react to customer needs. We lacked the controls and standard operating procedures to grow profitably.

Compression Planning helped us implement needed controls to strive to obtain our corporate vision, while living under our values and mission. With controls in place and the right team, we have had significant growth. Jerry McNellis and Compression Planning laid the groundwork to allow us to achieve our success."

Edward H. Schaefer
President/C.E.O.
Silver Spring Foods/Bookbinder Foods
Eau Claire, WI

"Compression Planning fell into my lap and I am glad it did. It has been, by far, the best professional development opportunity I have had in many years. The approach is fresh, sensible and credible – it works. I use this strategy in practically all aspects of my work...beyond formal Compression Planning sessions. In particular, I use it in planning trainings and meetings. I am using CP with a number of school districts in strategic planning or improvement planning.

I have used it with other groups as well to solve problems, kick-start stale plans and plan major events. The results of all my sessions have been surprisingly great. I am not sure why I continue to be surprised, but I do. People walk away from sessions thrilled with the product(s) generated – they love having a plan of action."

Dr. Judy Reault
Assistant Superintendent, Teaching and Learning
Educational Service District 123
Pasco, WA

'What People Say About Compression Planning'

"I estimate we complete projects in about a third less time with Compression Planning. The process allows us to be one of the most productive grants offices in the United States. There are only two staff members in our office, and last year we completed 188 projects. Over 22 years, we've received $118 million in successful grants. Compression Planning gives us a huge competitive edge. We use it on 100% of all major grants and projects.

We academics have a reputation for discussing things to death. We are exceptional at sitting around and admiring the problem. We want to look at all possible options, and end up solidly bogged down. Compression Planning enables us to avoid that and focus quickly on the key strategic things."

Neil Herbkersman
Senior Director of Grants Development
Sinclair Community College
Dayton, OH

"A one-day Compression Planning session to help a commercial aircraft flight software client 'focus its product value proposition' yielded – within three weeks of implementation – new contracts with the Sprint/Nextel corporate fleet, Honeywell, Worldspan, Goodrich, and Navaro giving an exponential leap for the small firm's revenues and long-term contracts.

The focused action plan from a one-day Compression Planning session helped a nonprofit foundation client achieve a 35% increase in annual donations within the first five months of its 12-month plan."

Brian Cubarney
Founder and Creative Director, ClearBrands, Inc.
Zelienople, PA

"Jerry McNellis has broken the code on focus and effectiveness in team planning. Compression Planning is the most effective collaboration tool that I have used – it builds teamwork, and simply gets things done. It is a gem of a tool for leaders who want to build collaborative teams, authentic consensus, and effective follow-through. Mastering this planning skill is well worth the effort.

If you want shorter meetings, authentic team consensus, and clear ownership and follow-through on tasks, Compression Planning is for you. Your team meetings will never be the same! (thank goodness!)"

Dan Chaverin
Executive Pastor
Westside Family Church
Lenexa, KS

"When a project needs collaboration, I know of no better way to define and establish that collaboration so that each partner takes ownership and feels good about her/his roll than using Compression Planning.

There is ALWAYS new, and sometimes surprising, information uncovered that strengthen one's application."

Blaise E. Favara, M.D.
South Valley Pediatrics & South Valley Child and Family Center
Hamilton, MT

"I have used Compression Planning for over 20 years at three companies. It is a great tool to bring people together to find an answer to anything from problems to vacation planning. When a team of people come together in this atmosphere and learn the method, they are unstoppable in finding and agreeing on a solution."

Les Whitver
Vice President, Michigan Seamless Tube
South Lyon, MI

"*Exploding the Meeting Myth* is the result of many years of experience, as Jerry McNellis has fine-tuned his breakthrough methodologies of how a leader can transform an organization and the process by which strategy is identified, planned and conducted (or implemented).

His concepts are focused, engaging of all, fun and highly effective in their capacity to produce results. I recommend his vision for organizational effectiveness – made practical in every sense of detail – to CEOs, division or department heads, planning executives, pastors, or anyone in a position to harness the help of others to

'What People Say About Compression Planning'

produce an end result. Jerry's methodologies are fresh and innovative, with the capacity to infuse an infectious form of energy into a team of people, whether it is a small group or large organization, wide-ranging or narrow in scope."

Bob Speck
President/CEO
Blue Coast Burrito
Brentwood, TN

"The CP Institute training was like turning a light on for me. I leaned the essential skills to become a more effective facilitator. I currently assist my company's internal strategic planning group by serving as a CP facilitator for a wide variety of cross-functional issues. I most recently used a CP session to help the Legal department to identify the formal processes and critical steps needed to manage contracts and legal documents. The goal was to prioritize the processes in order to more effectively introduce a document management information system.

The key concept I learned from CP is the importance of having a purpose, a non-purpose and background for each and every meeting. I have sat in too many meetings where time is wasted because every participant has a different idea of what is to be accomplished. CP teaches that getting everyone on the same page at the beginning of a meeting is essential if you are going to ask that group to address a topic or solve a problem."

Bryan A. Pai
Systems Analyst
SunEdison
Beltsville, MD

"I have experienced and used Compression Planning for over 25 years. How do you describe the indescribable – you don't – you need to experience it. If you get one message from this book, it must be 'I need to go and experience this!!'

From church retreat, to corporate board, to professional organization, to academic institution, to multiservice defense research project, to a family vacation – all are enhanced and enabled by this process.

The interactive and communication playing field is leveled as each participate – irrespective of rank or status – and has the opportunity for equal influence since the process ensures that ideas not individuals win the day and determine the future."

Trevor Macpherson M.D.
Professor of Pathology and Vice Chair Pathology
Medical Education
Residency and Fellowship Program Director
Department of Pathology
University of Pittsburgh Medical Center
Pittsburgh, PA

"In my role as Director of Planning and Grants at a large, public technical college, Compression Planning has been instrumental both in the development of an institution-wide strategic plan and in planning programs and grant projects. I have also successfully used Compression Planning with various smaller nonprofit organizations to develop program and fundraising action plans.

In every situation where I use this approach, people who participate are delighted with the outcomes they achieve in a short period of time, and they are always energized by the process and appreciate the relationships that emerge from this positive experience. And in the debriefing process, it's clear that people feel valued by having used their limited time wisely and productively. This is absolutely the best approach to planning I have seen in any organization!"

Sula J. Hurley
Director Office of Planning and Grants
Greenville SC Technical College
Greenville, SC

"Over the past 10 years, I have leveraged Compression Planning to drive powerful outcomes to critical decisions and thinking in both corporate and nonprofit environments. The logic behind the Compression Planning approach brings the best out in meeting participants in a transparent, democratic way. Some powerful insights have emerged from Compression Planning sessions.

The genius behind Compression Planning is much more than a unique way to facilitate meetings. Compression Planning starts by understanding the basic human needs

'What People Say About Compression Planning'

of recognition, certainty, variety, growth, contribution and connection. The secret sauce of Compression Planning is that it plays to basic human needs and builds on participant strengths.

I have found Compression Planning to be a welcome remedy to emotionally charged topics. It works again and again. Perhaps that's why I've had Jerry train numerous leaders and associates numerous times over the years."

Chris Padgett
Corporate Director of Marketing
Humana Inc.
Louisville, KY

"I was introduced to Compression Planning in 2005 and attended the Advanced Institute in 2008. If anything, I waited too long before attending the second meeting!

Compression Planning is truly a unique way of thinking and I have used it in developing mission, vision, values statements for both non-profit and for-profit organizations. Our clients have found the CP sessions to be both intuitive and energizing.

Intuitive in the sense that the structure and rules make complete sense, and energizing in the sense that they are cognitively liberating – enabling participants to take larger steps in thinking and decision-making in less time than they might otherwise."

David Fortt
Founder, New Image Associates
Tolland, CT

"We were hired by an area university to help with a problem they were stymied with. They tried to develop a specific program for two years, but they kept going around in circles. With one Compression Planning session, they were finally able to generate action steps that they had struggled to come up with for two years."

Dr. Morris Beverage
President
Lakeland Community College
Kirtland, OH

"I first encountered Jerry McNellis and his methodology for addressing issues while working for the General Motors EV1 program. The EV1 was an invention-on-demand program that required quick, thoughtful action to address problems, define alternatives and build electric vehicle solutions. Jerry's method for capturing ideas, focusing discussions and enhancing ideas to encompass more than simple thoughts provided the means for our team to define the future.

The Compression Planning process is simple to implement and results in team cohesiveness. It is so much easier to build the future with your team aligned to a common purpose. An action plan built with commitment to incorporate input from all players is a plan with a greater chance for success. This process provides that result.

I have personally utilized the process to determine my future career plans with great success. Jerry is a mentor I respect and admire who suggested that this approach could be used to capture the myriad of thoughts surrounding any subject including personal planning. I gave it a shot and it worked. I use it for everything from defining bylaws for a cabin community to next career positioning. Thank you, Jerry, for your enlightenment. I recommend that others take the opportunity to grow and try the process to clarify their world."

Laurel Castiglione
Former Manager, Web Governance, Globalization and Marketplace; Corporate Communications
General Motors Corporation
Proprietor, Castiglione Enterprises, LLC

"I was just trained in Compression Planning this last summer of 2008 during my year-and-a-half stay in the United States. Very enthusiastic about the concept and what I have learned, I was sure that it would not only work in the US but also in Europe.

The perfect occasion occurred when we had a retreat of our family-owned Forest Management Company 'Boscor Forest' that manages roundabout 30,000 acres of forest land in Germany and Austria. There were six forest engineers, three administrators, three members of the senior management team, plus me as the 'independent' facilitator. The goal was to identify critical issues in our

'What People Say About Compression Planning'

day-to-day business in the following areas: Forestry (Production), Administration and Management.

After a day-and-a-half of storyboarding and a lot of fun we came up with five key problems that we needed to address in the next year to improve our outcomes as well as detailed plans that outlined the action steps to solve each problem.

At first, the Germans were very skeptical. In the end, very enthusiastic about Compression Planning and what we had achieved: no more wood production without storyboarding!!"

Constantin von Reizenstein
Ph.D. Student in HealthCare Economics
University of Munich
Co-Owner of a German Forest Estate

"The logic of coordinated group problem solving is too often trumped by the associated burden. In *Exploding the Meeting Myth*, Jerry McNellis outlines a thoughtful process used successfully with countless organizations over three decades. The bottom-line is quicker and smarter answers that address fundamental organizational problems and opportunities.

But in the Compression Planning process so much more is gained. Learning with peers becomes a reality. The ability to see issues with clarity and to sift quickly through volumes of data and information is improved.

The process also highlights a key failure in organizational development—deciding what not to do. And importantly, the methods outlined can be used regularly throughout the year with efficiency and speed."

Steve Moya
Former CMO, Humana, Inc.
Santa Barbara, CA

"My husband Marc and I returned to the Philippines two weeks ago, and the first thing we did was to start a Compression Planning session. We had each gathered snippets of information from different sources on our two-month trip in the US, and wanted to share them as part of the background for our planning.

We then moved to our non-purposes, and sure enough there were about 10. We were left with the one thing we had to focus on as we returned. Within two hours we had defined our task, the parameters which needed to be met and within four days we had accomplished that goal and were ready to plan again.

It was the NONs that helped us focus and get complete agreement so quickly."

Suzanne Jacobson
Training Consultant
Manila, Philippines

"We'd been through a very difficult transition in our college, and felt the need to begin healing the institution. We decided that strategic planning was to be the vehicle for bringing people together, and we chose Compression Planning with Jerry McNellis as the model for our process. We trained 17 people as Compression Planning facilitators and this group evolved into the institution's Planning Council.

With Jerry's assistance, we conducted a series of external focus groups and ultimately, decided the best approach was to put every employee in the college through Compression Planning simultaneously. We did 14 sessions concurrently, for more than 300 people in one day. It was a way to demonstrate across the college that we were serious in our commitment to transform the institution and that we were serious about our employees being part of the process.

We were so pleased with the outcome that we now use Compression Planning in a variety of ways, other than just strategic planning for the institution. We're using it in work with our Advisory Committees, working with some of our internal committees and councils and in curriculum planning. We're starting to use it in work we do with some of the external organizations in our communities. We are adapting the process to our institution and are extremely pleased with the successes we are having.

We've given voice to a group of people who felt they did not previously have a voice in the organization. Compression Planning created a framework allowing us to address thorny issues in a positive, productive manner.

'What People Say About Compression Planning'

Very quickly, people realized they were being given power and they demonstrated their commitment by taking ownership of the process and outcomes. It kept them in an active role. We've had members of the staff stay they've never worked in an organization where they felt as valued as they do now. That's a powerful statement.

I've been in the administration of higher education for over 30 years. The day the Planning Council presented the Vision, Mission, Values and Goals developed through the Compression Planning process to the College's Board of Trustees was probably the single most emotional day in the life of an institution that I have seen in my career. I have never felt prouder of an organization in my life.

I knew intuitively there would be a strengthening of the institution resulting from our experience with Compression Planning. I don't think any of us expected the power, strength and commitment we've seen. We've gotten far more out of the experience than we anticipated. We're now in a good place and we're becoming a stronger institution through our work with Jerry and Compression Planning.

Trust the process of Compression Planning. At the end of the day, if you stay with the process, it will get you where you want to go."

Joe Forrester
President, Community College of Beaver County
Monaca, PA

"I used Compression Planning with our board to set priorities for the areas we would pursue for grants. Frequently working with such groups is like herding cats and CP helps rein them in and get people focused and committed.

CP helped make the ideas concrete/specific. It was an interdisciplinary group...academic and community members."

Joan Haley
SW Area Health Education Center & Coordinator
Pittsburgh Schweitzer Fellows Program
Pittsburgh, PA

"Compression Planning - A Million Dollar Idea

Dear Jerry,

Thank you so much for your Compression Planning seminar I attended last year at Robert Morris University. It has been helpful to me personally and professionally. As a result of that seminar, I've led several sessions in our company and your techniques have proven to be quite useful in helping us generate new marketing ideas.

You'll be interested to know that one idea that came out of one planning session helped develop an idea that generated over $1,000,000 with a single email promotion in less than a week.

I led a Compression Planning brainstorming meeting in Delray Beach, Florida with a few top level copywriters who work with me at Agora, Inc. Agora publishes financial analysis and advice for individual investors. The purpose of the meeting was to generate new headline and lead ideas for promotions. Out of that two-hour meeting came four ideas worth further development for our products.

One of the ideas that came from the brainstorming session was further developed by an editor/copywriter into a promotion for a $10,000 financial product to be sold via the Internet. That one promotion alone generated over 100 orders in less than a week. You do the math. That's over a million dollars.

This was an unusually successful promotion behind a very big idea for an expensive product. A typical email promotion may generate $35,000 to as much as $100,000. So this got a lot of attention. It didn't come without a lot of effort (and also a few headaches), but still the results were remarkable.

Since that planning session, there has been a much greater interest in using Compression Planning for other divisions of our company.

Thom Hickling (deceased)
Freelance writer for Agora Inc.

'What People Say About Compression Planning'

"Several things happened during my first CP session. First, even though I had always received compliments on my facilitation skills, I was taken aback by the participation of each group and how good they felt at the end of the sessions.

Second, we got twice as much accomplished than with my old process and no one left wondering about the next steps.

And, finally, we didn't have to figure out how one newsprint stuck on the wall related to another because the CP boards and cards were organized...they were right in front of us and easy to build on in preparing our next session and next proposal draft. I was sold!

I find the preplanning session with the key stakeholders invaluable. By having this session in place, the first session with multiple stakeholders is so much more productive and people participating really appreciate the clarity of the bigger picture.

We're using CP with every single proposal that we develop. I do know that we have improved the time it takes us to develop most grants by eliminating duplication of effort and not having to backtrack to find out something that we missed.

The 'old dogs' like me who have problems learning 'new tricks' need to know that this will bring a breath of fresh air to your work and you'll wonder where it has been all of your life. Just think about the fact that people will walk away feeling good about the meeting (how often does that happen?) and they will be talking about how skillful you are to others."

Judith Cawhorn
Executive Director of Grant Development
Mott Community College
Flint, MI

"It began innocently enough over two decades ago at a professional society retreat. The stated aim of said retreat was to update the society's strategic plan. Anticipating the usual fruitless and boring meeting with colleagues, I reluctantly agreed to participate. Two days later, the society had a new future roadmap, every participant was energized and engaged, and I was a changed person. The meeting was facilitated by Jerry McNellis and his colleagues from the Compression Planning Institute. It was my introduction to the power of the Compression Planning methodology.

Enthralled by the outcome of that meeting, I attended a training session determined to learn the basic principles. I returned to my home institution as an enthusiastic proponent. Within months I facilitated any number of disparate planning sessions – from re-designing the psychiatry department to exploring the hospital's role in fetal medicine. Each proved so successful that we invited Jerry to train a wider group of facilitators at the hospital. I have employed Compression Planning in such diverse settings as nonprofit organizations, schools, and professional groups, all the way to the personal level of selling our home.

Of all the tools and techniques I have learned over the years, the only one that has endured, matured and evolved to where it is as useful today as it was when I was first exposed to it, has been Compression Planning. It is adaptable to a wide variety of planning and problem solving issues. Regardless of the latest management fad du jour, Compression Planning can be employed with success."

Denis R Benjamin B.Sc., M.B.,B.Ch
Medical Director of Pathology and Laboratories
Cook Children's Medical Center
Fort Worth, TX

Past President – Society for Pediatric Pathology
(a.k.a. The Cowtown Curmudgeon)

'What People Say About Compression Planning'

"Compression Planning is the single most effective thinking strategy and group planning and problem solving technique I have ever learned. Learning the process profoundly changed the way I planned and thought through every part of my life. In the over twenty years I have been using the process I have led hundreds of group planning sessions around the country. Without exception attendees are amazed at how much gets accomplished in so little time and how fully engaged everyone is.

When I was hired as CEO I integrated the process into our way of doing business. Our staff are trained and we have trained and disseminated the technique to hundreds of people within our community and around the state. The return on investment in learning and using this process is so astronomical I can't even attempt to calculate it."

Luanne J. Panacek
Chief Executive Officer
Children's Board of Hillsborough County
Tampa, FL

"As a believer and user of Compression Planning, it has become a very valuable tool in our project management toolkit. We have adapted the CP structure and principles to the planning and execution of our IT projects. We have applied it in all phases of project management, including work breakdown sessions, daily team meetings, problem solving, and project retrospectives. The power of the tool for us is that:

- It provides a framework that is adaptable to a variety of applications.
- It creates a visual platform for information.
- It is persistent…we can work on it, stop, and come back to it. Team members can add things 'on-the-fly' for discussion with the group at a later time."

Jack R. Rearick, PMP
Project Management Office
Federated Services Company
Pittsburgh, PA

"Jerry and his team have done several strategic planning retreats for our clients, who are comprised of physicians and researchers primarily in academia. If any of our clients ever wants an outstanding, reasonably priced team to lead their strategic planning efforts, Jerry McNellis and Compression Planning are at the top of the list of our recommendations.

Jerry spends a fair amount of time interviewing participants in advance of the meeting, reading the association's literature, and is extremely prepared for the retreats. The design that goes into planning a retreat is so well thought out, and collaborative, that, in the end, we've always gotten a phenomenal product that has helped moved the organizations to the next level. The systems used are simply outstanding.

We recently had a retreat with Jerry and his team that involved some very complex issues. Jerry's firm, yet warm style, helped us work through these issues. And, it was actually quite fun in doing so! I consider Jerry a top-notch facilitator and a friend whom I highly respect."

Laura Degnon, CAE
Vice President, Degnon Associates
McLean, VA

"My very first reaction to reading the chapter on "'Pure Form Thinking"' and going through your course is that it is the cornerstone concept.

I thought that you detailed the various thought processes well and gave plenty of real-world suggestions and examples.

You always keep it real.

Reading the chapter brought me back to your session (almost live)."

William Safian
Director of Business Development
Advocate Health System/Trinity Hospital
Chicago, IL

'What People Say About Compression Planning'

"Sometime in the late 1970's, my boss sent me to a three-hour seminar with some guy named Jerry McNellis on Compression Planning. I was a typical frustrated Human Resources guy in an analytical, formal, engineering environment. The frustration came from the 'analysis paralysis' that such organizations fostered.

But Compression Planning became a real source of energy and personal motivation that has served my career and ambition very well for the last 30 years.

The analytical people in the organization came to love the process, its speed and its effectiveness. When I realized the impact this tool could have on organizations, it became my ticket to a truly unique career path as a professional facilitator with a product that really worked. And it worked every time.

Compression Planning has allowed me to build a business practice around strategic planning for boards of directors and trustees of major organizations and associations throughout the country. Since 1991, we've helped over 700 groups put together their strategies for future success.

When I think back, I didn't even want to go to that seminar."

Pete Clifford
President, Advanced Leadership Services
Columbus, OH

"On one level, *Exploding the Meeting Myth* by Jerry McNellis is a traditional 'how-to' business book, albeit an exceptionally well-written one. It compares favorably with the many business best sellers that I've read over the years. Each chapter has been researched well, there are many real-world examples of how to put his insights to use, and the reader is presented with lots of logical, thorough examples of how to take a simple business meeting and turn it into a series of actionable steps. Simply viewed as a 'how- to' manual, the book is a fine addition to any business library.

Like an onion, though, it has other layers beneath its surface. McNellis takes the reader on a journey. Early on in the book, it becomes very clear that he is the 'Yoda' of planning, facilitating, and mastering the

business meeting. Among the many thoughtful tips and observations, the reader also finds a straightforward commentary on 21st century business culture underlying the main message of this book. The message truly is insightful and, makes the book relevant to a wide audience. He takes on topics such as the team workplace, pureform thinking, how to focus on the real issues, and how to dig for rich ideas.

What I find most appealing about *Exploding the Meeting Myth* is how McNellis manages to integrate his interpretations in a way that prevents these important themes from becoming overbearing or preachy. He doesn't smack you over the head with his views; he simply guides you through some very insightful observations. Well done!"

Tedd Long
Principal, National Practice Leader
HR Innovation
Findley Davies, Inc.
Toledo, OH

"*Exploding the Meeting Myth* is a comprehensive and thoroughly enjoyable introduction to Compression Planning. It describes the ingeniously simple process that not only facilitates problem-solving, but also builds consensus and buy-in for even the most challenging issues.

Compression Planning has been an important tool in our firm's tool box for more than 20 years. We've used it to help clients design school buildings, plan promotional campaigns, facilitate a community investment plan for a major non-profit, and develop countless management strategies.

Author Jerry McNellis made his reputation as a highly stimulating and engaging presenter and facilitator. McNellis' personal observations and highly instructive case studies translate easily to the pages of *Exploding the Meeting Myth*. In highly readable style, this book provides a practical, real-world process for addressing virtually any issue with speed and clarity."

Mark Luetke
President, FLS Marketing
Toledo, Ohio OH

'What People Say About Compression Planning'

"Before receiving training in Compression Planning, I attended many meetings where the facilitator used this process. I found those meetings much more productive and focused, and with a pre-defined outcome when we completed our task.

My favorite part of Compression Planning is the communication plan.

It specifies the minute steps that the group must take to ensure that their plan is implemented with fidelity. It gives the group confidence that its hard work and wonderful ideas will actually be communicated, which adds accountability to ensure that the tasks will be completed!"

Carrie Bearden, Ph.D
Director of Exceptional Children
Ohio Valley Educational Cooperative
Shelbyville, KY

"Compression Planning is a 'spirit and energy audit' for leaders who will make a difference in their organizations. Jerry McNellis is the Yoda master of Compression Planning.

It's no secret now how he does it. Although he has his own magic to add, Jerry offers the Compression Planning Process for leaders who know that there is more they can give and more that their teams can give. Over the past twenty-five years, I have used this process and I know there is no better set of guidelines and concepts to develop teams and, generate plans, than Compression Planning. Every month, I use this process and I see the 'sprit and energy' of a team reemerge.

I know it works. I have worked with thousands of leaders, from corporations to religious communities to individuals who were spiritless and depleted of energy. This process brings an invitation to 'invest in the best ideas for the right reasons right here - right now.'

Compression Planning infuses confidence, sets direction, and in these scary financial times, Compression Planning provides the GPS way through the tough issues for organizations and leaders."

Nancy T. Foltz, Ph.D.
Pittsburgh, PA

"Compression Planning has played a role quietly behind the scenes of several initiatives over almost 20 years within Luxottica Retail (we're better known for our LensCrafters, Pearle Vision, Sunglass Hut, Sears Optical and Target Optical retail brands). We enlisted Jerry and his team years ago to help craft the early LensCrafters brand corporate mission, vision and core values; we've since used the process on multiple initiatives, from identifying streamlining opportunities to executing innovative ideas that delivered eyeglasses to more needy recipients during international optical missions. We've found Compression Planning very effective in taking initiatives from idea to action in a way that builds collaboration and consensus.

Luxottica Retail places heavy importance on leadership at all levels. As part of our leadership philosophy, we believe in challenging the process and enabling our associates to act. In a tough retail business climate, like other organizations we're faced with doing more, with fewer resources, in the least possible time. Once again, we've enlisted McNellis for high-impact workshops to help us equip a targeted pool of associates with Compression Planning skills. In a recent workshop, about 20 participants worked on real projects with an estimated price tag of almost $50 million. These participants, many with multi-million dollar business responsibilities, have begun to report powerful productivity gains. Some are moving projects forward by two months or more by conducting a single two-hour compression planning session.

Jerry McNellis and team have truly developed a 'thinking technology' that has proven effective for our organization over time, and now, we're incorporating it more than ever to empower associates, drive personal productivity, provide handrails for delivering results and developing leaders."

Annette Brown, Professional Development Specialist
Mary Pater, Director Talent Management
Luxottica Retail
Mason, OH

To my remarkable Mother

Helen McNellis

"The world's best listener"

What's Inside

INTRODUCTION - Blowing Fresh Life into What You're Doing - pages 1–3

Most managers instinctively know "what to do." Amazingly few know "how to do." This is a how-to-do book. It's about how to free up people so they can push and create new, winning concepts. It's about the Compression Planning Systems. This process helps leaders recruit and lead teams – turning ideas into practical action faster than they ever thought possible.

PART ONE
Putting the Process to Work

1. Leading Groups That Get Things Done Quickly - pages 4–6

Most decisive forces of competition are internal, not external. The imperative for managers, therefore, is to maximize the skills, time, and resources of their existing organizations. Compression Planning employs the best elements of planning and group dynamics, and enables teams to address virtually any issue with uncommon speed.

2. Pureform Thinking - the Cornerstone Concept - pages 7–13

Pureform thinking, the cornerstone concept of Compression Planning, separates the generation of ideas from the analysis and evaluation of those ideas. Most teams utilizing pureform thinking cut their planning time in half.

3. When to Use Compression Planning - pages 14–20

Use the Compression Planning Process any time people need to work as a team, move fast, and take action that is out of the ordinary. A list of 100 sample projects for Compression Planning will help you get started.

4. The Planning Specialist - pages 21–25

Compression Planning specialists have two principal functions on team projects: design the project and facilitate group sessions. Six key roles and 10 characteristics of planning specialists are examined. (Design is covered in Chapter 10).

5. The Centered Life of a Facilitator - pages 26–27

To be an effective facilitator requires skills, which can be learned and mastered; sensitivity, which must be nurtured; and intuition, which can be trusted.

6. How to Recruit High-Performance Teams - pages 28–33

If you are looking for a potent plan to solve a problem or seize an opportunity, select a potent team. Six proven steps will guide you in selecting the most effective team. A simple formula will help you determine group size.

7. Essentials for a Team Workplace - pages 34–238

The best locations provide an environment in which team members can be "fully present." Without distractions, individuals can focus 100 percent on an issue until the team has constructed concepts and committed to an action plan. A comprehensive guide tells how to select and equip planning rooms and how to work with conference center personnel.

PART TWO
How to Design and Lead a Planning Session

8. Storyboarding: All-at-Onceness Thinking - pages 39–41

Compression Planning employs a comprehensive version of the storyboarding process developed by Walt Disney Studios for planning films and theme parks. With storyboarding high-performance leaders encourage participation, protect ideas, and compress time out of team projects.

9. Master Compression Planning Model - pages 42–44

This schematic of the McNellis Master Planning Model for Compression Planning is the leader's guide for designing and pacing sessions. The model serves as the planning pattern and is used as a progress reference during the session.

10. Seven Steps to Effective Designs - pages 45–59

Each of the seven steps in the "session design form" is explained and examined. A great facilitator with a poor design will get so-so results. An average facilitator with a great design can get extraordinary results.

11. How to Focus on the Real Issue - pages 60–62

Three steps in the design stage – Overall Project Purpose, Session Purpose, and Non-Purpose – push the team to focus energy on what they propose to accomplish. Tight purposing energized a Michigan radio station to increase sales by 400 percent during one target month, and a hospital management team to cut personnel costs by 30 percent.

12. Format Designs for Most Projects - pages 63–71

Fifteen sample groups of headers are provided to address everyday issues tackled by project teams, with designs to aid novice and veteran facilitators.

13. How to Dig for Rich Ideas - pages 72–76

Spinning is the technique that helps planning groups reach beyond the first statement of an idea. The facilitator leads the team to build on, enhance, and give energy to ideas that can be forged into action.

14. Try the Squid, You May Like It - pages 77–80

The superstars in business don't do what others do in the way others do it. They strive for the unique factor, which implies energy, excitement, efficiency, and effectiveness. Grey Poupon discovered the unique factor in marketing mustard. Marriott Hotels developed unique systems for serving a hot breakfast in your room when you want it.

15. How to Warm Up Groups and Keep Them Hot - pages 81–85

The Compression Planning System, because it is designed to keep the team focused and moving, is itself an energizer. Here is a collection of techniques, tips, and aids to pick up the pace and reenergize a group.

16. Forging Clear Concepts from Rich Ideas - pages 86–88

In the focus phase of Compression Planning, the task is to sort through all ideas and fix on the keepers, those that will move the project forward. "Dotting" and other sorting techniques are explained and evaluated.

17. Put the Focus on What Must Be Done - pages 89–91

A simple organization storyboard is designed to help the team commit to action on its plan and to keep its commitment alive. The focus is on those few "must" tasks for the plan to succeed, nailing down individual commitments, and setting realistic deadlines as well as expected results.

18. Spreading the Word - pages 92–94

Informing others in the organization is integral to compression team plans. The communications plan is constructed in a grid format on a storyboard, where it can be seen as a whole. Content, target audiences, schedule, and responsibility are all spelled out.

**PART THREE
When You Are the Leader**

19. Lessons We Have Learned - pages 95–98

Experience and advice from a seasoned Compression Planning specialist: Start slowly. Go easy. Be realistic in your expectations.

20. Bear Traps and Final Thoughts - pages 99–101

The authors' greatest reward will be that, after reading this book, you will be better equipped to lead teams that want to make a difference. Too many important things need to get done not to give it a try. If you lead effectively, you will make a difference. You will grow and others will grow with you.

Introduction - Blowing Fresh Life Into What You're Doing

A senior executive confessed to me, "I've served on a task force for 16 months and we have done nothing but meet. We have no better understanding of our issue than when we started."

An educator serving on a statewide planning commission of 20 people related a similar story: "We met two days every other month for three years before we came up with a plan all of us could buy into."

These are not stupid people. They are not lazy bureaucrats. Their stories are not unusual. They hunger for a way of working together that will recognize and engage their potential, creativity, collaborative work, and bottom-line results.

This incredible need was driven home by an astute executive in one of America's biggest corporations. He had just been handed a new business unit that generated billions of dollars in annual revenues. Although he came to this new responsibility with lots of experience, he still asked himself, "How can I get my people moving in the same direction? This division in the corporation was once more profitable than any other. Then it went out of control. Our financial performance stinks. My job is to turn it around."

Gazing out a draped window of his high-rise corner office, he continued, "We've got to work like people who share a vision and are committed to getting there. Our jobs depend on how well we do and how fast we do it."

Every organization has remarkable resources stifled and bottled up. Unrecognized and unused, these represent creative talents and energies of people. Not just the leaders. Not just the most visible. Not just the few. Everyone! No

organization today can afford anyone on the payroll not used to his or her full potential.

When it comes to tapping creative talents and energies of people, most managers instinctively know "what to do." Few know "how to do." This book embraces the following: How to free up people so they can push out fresh, new ideas and create new, winning concepts. It's meant to be a "bible" on how to lead teams so they can turn ideas into bottom-line results faster than they ever imagined possible.

When I was growing up, I didn't hear a lot of "No, that won't work." Dad was a research chemist and he would say, "Let's try." Outside of my home – in high school, college, part-time jobs – it was a different story. I heard "No" lots of times. Experimenting was not encouraged. Often it wasn't even tolerated. We were instructed and tested for the "right answers."

Not until my first job out of college did I learn what most adults do for a living. They go to meetings! I spent endless hours in ill-conceived, poorly planned and ineptly led meetings. We would discuss an issue but things were seldom resolved! People rejected most new ideas out of hand, saying, "That's crazy. We've never done it that way." Or someone would say, "Management won't buy that. No way!"

My second job was assistant manager of the Chamber of Commerce in Austin, Minnesota. I went to lots of meetings there, too. Often I would come away sick, wondering why smart people wasted so much time. We never got around to real issues such as: What are we about? Where are we going? How are we going to get there? What can I contribute? We never asked these tough questions, so we seldom addressed anything that mattered.

Leaders assumed simply calling a meeting could get individuals to plan as a team, solve problems, and make decisions. I soon realized for me to ever find satisfaction in a job, this meeting myth had to be exposed. In frustration, I began to search for new ways to work with groups and try new meeting formats and leadership styles. I attended seminars, scoured magazines, read books, and talked with anyone who might have a new idea.

My search took me to a seminar on Creative Thinking, in which Mike Vance described a planning concept he helped develop during his time with the Walt Disney organization. This was different! At Disney, they captured ideas by printing them on cards they then pinned on storyboards. Then a team selected ideas with high potential and turn them into those fabulous cartoons and movies we all loved as kids and now watch on television. Today, storyboards embody a worldwide standard for planning all manner of visual communications.

Vance laid out an intellectual framework for creative thinking and taught me to use storyboards as my working medium. With this approach, people plan and work together with new freedom, knowing they won't be clobbered when their ideas differ. Storyboarding encourages creativity and gets everybody involved because it protects ideas and egos.

Every seminar and planning session I've led since 1973 has had one constant: to pay tribute to Mike Vance for his special willingness to help me at a crucial time in my development. I've gained many of these thoughts from Mike. I hope this book and the work of the people of The McNellis Company serve as a tribute to him and his Uncle John.

Seeds of creativity planted by my father and nurtured by Vance have grown and matured through hundreds of planning sessions I've led over many years. Out of this total experience emerged what we call "The McNellis Compression Planning System." With this method for collaborative work, groups have a high-speed, systematic procedure for generating ideas and forging rich concepts they can use to make things happen.

People who go through our Institute learn the Compression Planning System. They learn to resolve in hours or days issues that could drag on for weeks and months in many organizations. Teams ranging in size from a handful of individuals to hundreds of people have achieved amazing results.

For example:
- Two Wisconsin corporations resolved an issue in three days that had festered for 18 months and threatened to abort their merger.
- After two years of regular committee meetings had failed to reach a consensus, child welfare laws of a mid-western state were rewritten in two Compression Planning sessions.
- In one day, some 150 managers and supervisors of a large communications company put energy and commitment behind a strategy to shave $1.5 million from costs over a 12-month period.

For years, people have been asking me what has been written on the subject of The McNellis Compression Planning System. Literature searches have produced little more than brief mentions here and there.

So Jack Nettles and I decided to write this book, which is for executives, managers, and professionals searching for better ways to stimulate, capture, and focus the creative energies of working groups.

Many people have been influential in my life. I would like to thank all of them at some point in this book, but space is limited and I would miss someone special. Those who know me best also understand this would be an overwhelming emotional experience for me. I make one exception, however. My son Pat and his wife Stephanie are key teammates in our company. They are a delight to work with and a constant source of support and joy.

When I first started in this business, I was referred to Jack Nettles when he managed corporate communications at Alcoa. We hit it off at our first meeting. Jack came to our second Compression Planning Institute and put it to work with energy and imagination. I liked and respected Jack as a person and was impressed with the clarity and crispness of his writing. Later, he retired from Alcoa and we joined as teammates in developing this book. Later on Pat McNellis and Scott Lowe became part of the team to bring this subject to life in this book.

We've tried to capture and pass on lessons learned from my father, Mike Vance, thousands of people in our Compression Planning Institutes, and from some more than three decades of pro-fessional facilitating of Compression Planning sessions for clients. I hope this book speaks to another Jerry McNellis who's just beginning to realize life is a collaboration.

As you read Exploding the Meeting Myth, you will notice some pushpins here and there. They're used to identify sections worthy of emphasis and have something in particular I want you to remember.

Chapter 1: Leading Groups That Get Things Done

An elusive insight into any organization today is the recognition that most decisive forces are internal, not external. How well people think, work, and create together invariably is more crucial than the competition's whiz bang new technology, computer integration, or government subsidy.

I talk with people almost every week in companies where internal friction consumes massive amounts of human energy. The culture suppresses creativity, stalls decision making, and discourages action. Bitter disputes between rival factions, though cleverly concealed and publicly denied, sap the vitality of the entire organization. While the battle rages inside, the competition goes unchallenged outside.

This is the norm, but it is not the whole. Every day I work with leaders who encourage new ideas from any source. Often they manage pockets of innovation and risk-taking in organizations not otherwise known for their stretch. These leaders value people and give them room and support. They spin ideas and drive for unique answers that distance their teams from the pack.

Conventional wisdom would have us believe that Company A guns down Corporation B in the marketplace. Yet the evidence is overwhelming that the losers shoot themselves. They are so exhausted by internal battles, they have little time or ammunition to engage the marketplace.

The big prizes of competition are won by organizations rooted in the fundamentals of their business, aligned in their goals, and focused enthusiastically on the crucial issues. Every area of the business, internal and external, is aimed at serving customers. Winning teams work together, with systems and skills that maximize their time and resources.

 The Compression Planning System helps groups work together creatively to get more done in a shorter time than they ever thought possible.

Ideas borne of creativity are wrapped in the fragile tissue of personal ego. People desperately need to have their ideas heard. Many times they are not saying, "Do my ideas," they are simply asking that their ideas be considered.

In Compression Planning, ideas and other information are recorded on index cards that groups pin to four-foot-square storyboards. With one card for each idea or element of information, groups can easily add new material, change their minds, regroup ideas, generate plans, and set priorities in a search for the elegance of a few unique factors done uncommonly well. This is the environment in which people collaborate to create strategies that win in global competition.

The key to understanding Compression Planning is to recognize it's a structure that combines the best elements of planning into a methodology that can be used to address almost any issue. Compression Planning enables project teams to move with uncommon speed to the benefit of their company and themselves.

TAPPING THE FULL POTENTIAL

Recently, the CEO of a corporation told me, "I want to put my key officers together to write a scenario for the future. I'm hesitant, though. When we get together, they say very little. They never have ideas that are creative or daring.

Could they be afraid to tell me and each other what's on their minds?" He looked into my eyes and added, "These folks are too bright, and they are making too much money to act like this. We must function as a team, but I don't know how to do it."

He asked me to design a Compression Planning Strategy Conference for his senior staff. After the retreat, he wrote me a letter in which he said, "The session far surpassed my expectations. Those guys had more ideas than I ever imagined. Good ideas, creative ideas. We worked fast. We worked as a team."

I can hardly believe that anyone can rise to such a high executive position in any organization today without the skills of effective team leadership. Yet, it happens. Michael Doyle and David Straus suggest a reason in their book, *How to Make Meetings Work*. "There is a big difference," they write, "between understanding how to make meetings work and actually making them work better."

Compression Planning, in its fundamental form, is exquisitely simple. In practice, it is more complex. These are the four basics for effective compression planning work:

- **ONE CLEARLY DEFINED TOPIC** is the rule. Although defining the topic is often difficult, it's always a critical step in the process.

- **THE SPONSOR/CLIENT** is the person who "owns" the project. The client recruits the facilitator, invites team members, and sponsors the activity.

- **THE TEAM** is composed of individuals who have a stake in the issue, or have a unique experience or knowledge to contribute. The group creates the action plan and, in most cases, is responsible for its success.

- **THE FACILITATOR** is experienced in group process and trained in the Compression Planning System. He designs the session and leads the group. The facilitator may be from outside the organization, an employee, or even a member of the group, but he should always be aware of his responsibility as facilitator and not get buried in content.

FOOTNOTE

Incidentally, because no neutral, first-person singular pronoun graces the English language, we will use the male gender in odd numbered chapters and the female in even chapters, unless a specific person is named or implied.

TERMINOLOGY

Important terms you should become familiar with:

STORYBOARDING

Storyboarding is the working medium of the Compression Planning System. All proceedings – the project design, ideas, concepts, and plans – are printed on index cards of various sizes and colors, and then pinned to the four-foot-square storyboards. Storyboarding fills the basic need of groups for "all-at-onceness thinking"; that is, the ability to see the whole of an issue while still dissecting and reshaping its parts. Storyboarding is fast and flexible. By moving cards, the group

5

can restructure its thinking while still developing ideas.

PUREFORM THINKING

The team divides its work into two phases: exploration and focus. In the exploration phase, they create, search, explore, uncover, and discover ideas that yield solutions. The focus phase is the time for analysis, judgment, and selection. These two phases are separated by a time break in the proceedings.

FOCUSED ENERGY

This is the driving power of Compression Planning. For a specified time, the group directs all of its energy to the issue.

COMMITMENT TO RESOLUTION

Going into the session, the team agrees it will emerge with a clear plan of action within a set period of time.

The key concepts and procedures taught in our Compression Planning "laboratory" / Institutes are here. No book, of course, can capture the give-and-take experience that comes from working in a group tackling real-life issues. Ultimately, everyone learns by stepping out and taking a chance. The basics and many of the fine points required to make Compression Planning work for you are covered in this book, which is divided into three parts:

PART ONE: Putting the Process to Work suggests areas in which Compression Planning can work for you. It supplies you with the background you need to understand and work in the compression mode.

PART TWO: How to Design and Lead a Planning Session is your handbook for leading groups. The Master Planning Model will guide you through design sessions and leading teams to accomplish more in a shorter period than you ever thought possible.

PART THREE: When You Are the Leader is drawn from my 30+ years of experience as a designer and facilitator of Compression Planning sessions. It is filled with the kind of stories seasoned facilitators tell each other at the end of a hard day. These are the stories that begin, "I'll never forget..." and "Have you ever..."

6

Chapter 2: PureForm Thinking - The Cornerstone Concept

Pureform thinking is a cornerstone concept in Compression Planning. It separates two distinct thought processes: creative and analytical. A facilitator must understand and practice pureform thinking to design and lead effective teams.

CREATIVE   ANALYTICAL

Mixing

CREATIVE THINKING

With our creative thought process, we accept new ideas. We search, explore, probe, uncover, and discover. In creative thinking, individuals accept new ideas, much as my family and I accepted foreign students at a party sponsored by a local chapter of American Field Service (AFS). We met students from many different countries, young people with different traditions, viewpoints, and physical appearances. Most American kids were dressed in shorts, tank tops, and blue jeans. Foreign students came in their traditional dress. A variety of foods were there for us to sample. Our role was to entertain these people and learn from them.

In the exploratory stage of pureform thinking, you don't reject ideas, you accept them as stated. Ideas at this stage are neither good nor bad. In most settings, if an idea appears bold or fresh, it's greeted with a barrage of critical phrases and a smattering of analytical judgment. Someone may imply or say, "That's a really dumb

idea and you're pretty stupid for suggesting it." Or you may offer your prize idea and in return get a look that seems to ask, "Were your mother and father ever on a first-name basis?" In the creative phase of Compression Planning, you help people understand how to participate and encourage them to hold analytical and judgmental thinking for the focus phase of your session.

ANALYTICAL THINKING

With our analytical thought process we judge, select, and evaluate. This demonstrates the rational mind's functions of linear, logical, sequential thinking. It's how most of us function most of the time. We can't get along without analytical thinking. How else would we ever find our way from one side of town to another, fly an airplane, or read this book for that matter? Analytical thinking comes from a little voice inside your head saying, "This doesn't make sense," when you see something outside the context of your view of reality. Our analytical minds often reject ideas perceived as unique. They appear illogical, almost senseless.

In Compression Planning we divide analytical thinking into pure analytical and critical analytical. Pure analytical is characterized by "We tried this 25 times and here is our experience." We know your concept works or doesn't work, based on real-life testing and experience. This demonstrates the scientific method: set a hypothesis, test it, and loop back with your results. This is "pure" analytical thinking.

Critical analytical thinking comes out as: "That's a dumb idea and you're a jerk for suggesting it" (or the implication of the latter). "We have never tried that before" (which is reason enough not to do it now). We all recognize these comments as "destructive phrases." They can be pure analytical, as opposed to critical analytical, and still be deadly. Killers tend to be ways of saying, "This is outside my view of reality or understanding, therefore it's wrong or, at best, unworkable."

In the analytical phase of Compression Planning sessions, you look for crisp judgment, selection, and analysis based on reflection. You want to give an idea a chance rather than make an early snap judgment. All of us must make a zillion judgments a day, judgments such as whether to brush our teeth, reorganize a department, introduce a new product, prepare dinner, or go out to eat. In a Compression Planning session, you compress time and postpone judgment during the process by agreeing to delay judgment on every idea. Get all of your ideas, options, and approaches out, then judge them. No matter how much time you spend analyzing, you have avoided instant rejection. And you have avoided negating an idea with a harmful phrase.

SOME FAULT-FINDING PHRASES - Turn-offs for new ideas

- It's not in the budget
- We're not ready for it
- Too hard to administer
- Everybody does it this way
- Production won't accept it
- Too theoretical
- Personnel isn't ready for this
- Not timely
- The old timers won't use it
- The new people won't understand it
- Takes too much time
- Don't move too fast
- Has anyone else ever tried it

- Let's do a market test first
- Let's form a committee
- Won't work in our territory
- Too big (or too small) for us
- We don't have the manpower
- We tried that before
- Too academic
- It's a gimmick
- You'll never sell that to management
- Stretches the imagination too much
- Let's wait and see
- Too much trouble to get started
- It's never been done before
- The union will scream
- Let's put it in writing

Pureform thinking is great in theory. It sounds wonderful. And it works! But it is difficult to practice because we have so many prejudices, so much data and so much experience. We carry in our minds so many formulas of "the way it should be," many people find it difficult even to hear new ideas.

While sitting in a group, you may hear someone say, "The way we ought to drive costs out of this product is to eliminate xyz system," and you may be the one who developed the system she is attacking. This triggers a reaction not analytical but critical: "You don't know enough. Who are you?" Killer responses can pour out in spite of your best intentions.

To deal with this kind of natural reaction, Compression Planning teams negotiate ground rules at the beginning of your session. They agree to suspend judgment of ideas during an exploration phase. During your focus phase, they need to judge ideas, but not people. Without this pureform approach, most groups mix creative and analytical thinking. They tend to move slowly, seldom realize breakthroughs with unique solutions, and often fail to find answers to their problems.

SOME "FAULT-FINDING" FACES

You've seen these, and many others. But you see how these faces can change the mood of a session, intentionally or unintentionally. So treat "Fault-finding Faces" as you would "Fault-finding Phrases." Be aware of your group dynamics.

In my years of working off this pureform model, I have yet to see a group who couldn't become more creative and engage in higher-level thinking when others stopped shooting holes in what they were doing while they were doing it. Ideas are delicate, especially in the early stages. People can't take harsh evaluation and criticism. This kind of talk in many political campaigns turns us off. The candidates blast away at each other and rarely come up with new thinking of their own. Why? To avoid getting riddled in return or because they have nothing original to contribute. It's easy to shoot holes in somebody else's ideas, but making those ideas useful is tough.

Building a Supportive Team

In Compression Planning, we design an arena in which people can put their energy into building ideas. If you introduce an idea and I try to enhance it, build on it, and turn it into a useful concept, you see me as an ally. If someone attacks my idea right away, I become defensive, withdraw, and may offer no more thoughts. If I do come out with ideas, I may come on so strong I may be obnoxious.

Your group benefits from neither the withdrawal nor the attack approach. Let's get the ideas out, dig for the truth, explore, think them through, and then make judgments and selection. To be productive, group members need to know where the group thinking is: Are we in the creative, generative, developmental, exploration phase? Are we over on the judicial, selective, analytical, logical stage of our work?

Like most people who read this book, you may come out of a discipline saying logic is good. So do I. But what kind of logic are we talking about?

In our Compression Planning Institutes, I joke about a guy I used to work with at summer camp. He would take a shower and then dry his left foot, his left leg, and so on until he had finished drying the left side of his body. Then he would get dressed on the left side. He would repeat this process on his right side. I watched him and thought he was nuts. His way of dressing was outside my view of reality. It wasn't logical to me but he got dressed and it became no big deal.

Pureform thinking is relaxing, because you say to yourself, "I may hear ideas I don't like and don't agree with, but I am going to look for what's useful in them." This is similar to the "nature model" in procreation. How many sperm are launched to fertilize one egg? Millions! When it comes to ideas, most groups allow "one sperm and one egg." That's all you get!

When you study the Great Ones in anything, you find they experiment a lot and give themselves the freedom to mess around with something. This is what pureform thinking does. It says there's a time to be clean and tidy, and there's a time to mess around, experiment, probe, dig, and see what we can find, uncover, create. With pureform thinking, you're allowed to let go and discover what happens in your brain.

Not to complicate the concept, but to tap its full potential, sometimes you explore analytically. The rules of suspended judgment apply here, too. Exploring is not the time for me to challenge your evaluations. Let's get them out and see what we can learn. Get the exploration out fast, without requiring continuous justification and explanation of the details and nuances. People who make an effort toward pureform thinking say, "Instead of shooting ideas down, I'll see if I can enhance them." People who do this make better judgments. They have more data.

My oldest son, Patrick, spent a year of high school study in Venezuela. His studies began 10 months earlier when he said, "Dad, can we talk?" All of his friends were selecting colleges, but Pat hadn't made one visit. I was leaning on him, asking, "Pat, where are you going to college? When are we going to visit some campuses?" When we were alone, he said, "Dad, will you just hear me through on this idea?" He put me into a state of pureform thinking when he said, "I would like to repeat my senior year in high school."

My internal response was, "Pat has good grades in high school and he wants to re-do his senior year?" You can imagine how this violated my sense of logic. He didn't use these words, but he communicated: "Will you just listen? Will you at least entertain the idea?" He wanted to study in another country, as an American Field Service student.

"I don't know where I will be going," he said. "I don't know what language. But I want to have this experience." I could have made a snap judgment and said, "What a great idea!" or "Why would you want to do something like that?" and trivialized what Pat had been carrying inside himself while he worked up his nerve to ask his parents for their support.

Another possibility was to do as I did and say, "Let's explore this idea." This was not an easy reaction for me. I had to talk myself into it. The more data I received, the more information we had to make a judgment (versus a critical evaluation), the more logical a choice became. I have come to believe this was one of the greatest things we could have done for Patrick. This was one of the most important experiences of his life.

Similar situations occur in every phase of our lives. The chairman of the board of a multi-billion-dollar corporation said to me: "I must find a way to get better ideas out of my people. It is not that they don't have ideas. They are too intimidated to put them out in front of each other and in front of me."

These people fly around in corporate jets and lead exotic lives. If they have those kinds of hesitations, how about us? Who wants to be ridiculed? Who wants to be laughed at? When you take my idea and put it down harshly, critically, you attack me. However, if you protect the ideas and the people connected to them, you get higher quality thinking. People love to work in an environment like this. They thirst for it because their creativity can flourish.

I don't believe there are creative and noncreative people. This is theologically unsound and psychologically unbalanced. Some people haven't used their creativity for a long time. Study history and you will realize advancement comes from creative breakthroughs. This is true in art, drama, manufacturing, engineering, design, whatever. If this topic intrigues you, read *Lateral Thinking* by Edward de Bono, published by Penguin Books. He doesn't use the same terminology, but he advances the same concept.

I have been reading de Bono since he first started publishing, but the greatest pureform thinking influence in my life was my dad. As a research chemist, this kind of thinking was ingrained in his brain. He knew the only way you can really know the value of an idea is to test it.

Giving Your Creativity a Chance

My parents demonstrated this concept as I was growing up. I contracted polio when I was 2 1/2 years old and underwent more than a dozen operations on my legs and back over the following ten years. Neither Dad nor Mother put any curbs on me because, they said, I would learn from trying. I was an absolute hellion, allowed to play football or whatever I wanted to do. My parents had to go with me at the start of each new school year in the primary grades because teachers wanted to make special compensations for me.

Dad and mom told them, "Let him figure out how to do things. If he can't, he will tell you. Then you can help. But don't tell him he can't play kickball with other kids at recess. Let him try. He'll know if he can do it or not. There will be things he can't do, but a lot of things he will be able to do if you give him the chance."

I grew up with a "give-it-a-chance" mentality. So it's not something I have only read in books and heard at seminars. It's something I have lived since my earliest conscious years. I was allowed to try things I wouldn't be courageous enough to allow my own children to do under similar circumstances.

I can't imagine letting my child in a full-length leg cast climb a 40-foot tree. I fell out of such a tree. But I look at my spirit and energy today and know a lot of it comes from the fact I wasn't clamped down. I don't hold myself up as a model, but for me, those were learning experiences for life.

That's what happens with people. You must steer their energy and focus it to some degree. However, I see people so bound up and puckered, they are paralyzed by the fear of looking bad or being ridiculed. The reverse should be the norm. The bolder an idea, the more you should relax. Give bold ideas time to mature. It is better to accept or reject ideas after careful consideration than to find out our competition thought of it, analyzed it, tried it, and it worked! It is much better to say we chose not to do it rather than to say we didn't even allow it to be considered.

Today's practice of building consensus means allowing people to think. We must have great tolerance for other viewpoints. Engineering accepting manufacturing. Manufacturing accepting finance. It is not acceptable to say just because some teams differ from us they are wrong. We must try to find the usefulness. We also must acknowledge a lot of stupid ideas come our way and they ought to be treated as such in the analytical phase.

One of my most memorable speaking experiences was with a group from Jazzercise. After working with so many corporate executives and professional managers, to be working with 180 Jazzercise instructors was an energizing experience. I should have paid them. I explained pureform thinking one evening, and the next day during a break, one woman took me aside and showed me a letter she had written to her husband overnight. It went something like this:

Dear Charlie:
After hearing this presentation on Compression Planning and the whole idea of separating creative thinking from the analytical, I realize I probably have never given you more than three seconds on an idea before I put it down. I have been exceedingly skilled at blasting your ideas out of the sky. As I think about you now, I see the pain in your eyes. My promise to you is every time you present an idea from now on, I'll spend 15 minutes trying to figure out what is useful in your idea and how to help you make it work. This is my promise to you, Charlie.

She had recognized herself as a shoot-'em-in-the-ego person. Her closing comment to me was, "This may be the one thing that saves our marriage."

In your personal life, watch for things you may be critical of, and watch how you respond to new ideas. I think most adults can accomplish this with conscious effort. At our deepest level, people say, "Consider my idea. Just give it a chance." An idea may not be usable, but it can lead to something else usable.

I am convinced teams practicing pureform thinking can cut their working time by 50 percent. We recommend groups develop ideas enough so what gets pinned on your storyboard is useful and not just the first words out of somebody's mouth. When your team is ready to analyze, they have everybody's ideas from which to select.

Storyboarding is a useful medium for helping individuals release their ideas. Putting an idea on a card on your storyboard moves it into the group domain. If we accept your idea, we accept you.

Storyboarding allows a group to suspend attention. Your group can go off to something and then come back from that something and resume storyboarding where they left off. Whereas by just talking without good, shared documentation, key thoughts can be lost. When an idea is represented visually, it also can be linked to other ideas for further development.

Ideas...Handle with Care
One of my most profound learning moments came in the final session of a two-day planning retreat involving the top staff of a huge corporation. We had hung 30 storyboards filled with ideas and were sorting through cards, making judgments and selections. In the final 30 minutes, I took a card off a board, casually dropped it on the table, and said, "I guess this doesn't fit." Even then I knew there is a big difference be-

tween "This doesn't fit what we are doing" and "This isn't a useful idea."

The financial person in the group said, "You took a rather cavalier attitude toward my idea." He was one of the brightest in the group. This was a moment of truth for him – and for me. His idea had come out in a flurry of ideas. I don't know how he could have even tracked it. Nobody else remembered where it came from. Yet, after we had gone through hundreds of cards, I tossed one card, and I could see he was insulted.

I don't do that anymore. I take cards one by one and say to the group, "Does this fit?" If they conclude a card doesn't fit, I put it in an enve- lope pinned to the storyboard marked "Re- trieval." Ideas are not discarded; I set them aside for possible consideration later.

Mike Vance told me Walt Disney often ex- plored trash cans after everyone else had gone home to retrieve ideas which had been tossed out. He returned them for evaluation, study, and judgment. Some of the most creative ideas were found among the discards.

In flattened organizations in which many of us work, there's little opportunity to move out of a contentious environment. We must invent ways to be supportive of each other. If somebody kicked you in your head 10 years ago, you remem- ber. Pureform thinking will not be a cure-all for every hurt, but it helps parry some painful shots to the ego.

Chapter 3: When To Use Compression Planning

The Duke of Wellington, a heroic English general and prime minister, was said "to think of the shoes of his soldiers." He paid attention to details, knowing if he overlooked small things such as the shoes of the soldiers, his major strategies would never work out. The same can be said of today's stand-out leaders in business, government, and other organizations. In the axiom of Wellington, the good ones consider "the shoes of their soldiers."

I have noticed over the years some leaders save Compression Planning for the "big things." Some have lamented, "Why didn't I use it in the little things? Why didn't I use it to 'watch the shoes of the soldiers'?"

Compression Planning doesn't work in every situation, but don't wait for your 100-year flood. Use it any time you need to work together, move fast, and produce action out of the ordinary. Our clients have used the process to plan a factory of the future, rewrite a state's welfare laws, organize a convention, and design a move from one office to another.

One day, my former teammate Dick Schultz took a phone call from his friend Craig MacFarlane, who was called the world's greatest blind athlete. Craig was invited to appear on Robert Schuler's "Hour of Power" television program. He was leaving for the California taping in two days and wanted help in thinking through his appearance.

Dick's schedule was crowded so they met over lunch and a pad of storyboard forms using the basic design template. They used clear, crisp thinking to build the pivotal ideas, weed out extraneous materials, and anticipate questions Dr. Schuler might ask. In 20 minutes they had a plan. Craig later tape-recorded the essence of their planning to review during his flight to California.

Use Compression Planning When You Must Move Quick

Compression Planning is made for action-kinds of people. Your commitment and expectation is we're getting together not "to talk about" an issue, but to create, build, resolve and deliver. We expect results. We plan for and commit to action.

 Compression Planning tackles what may consume eight hours and does it in two hours. If you need quickness, that's one of the drivers. If you need thoroughness, it will do thoroughness faster. It will do creative faster. It will do team building faster.

We were called in by a client who was working on designing a corporation's factory of the future. "We've been talking about this project for months," he explained. "We've been theorizing, drawing one scheme after another. Now it's time to cut the bacon and get something moving." He expected his team to spend four months preparing a proposal. Instead we designed a session, and a team of 14 engineers and senior managers conceived a plan in one and one-half days. Their proposal was done in hours rather than months.

A front-end decision on a project like this is "Let's not sit and talk about it. Let's agree on a plan and make it happen." You design your planning session so when people walk in, they can operate in a compressed mode. They use simple ground rules and a neutral facilitator to move the process along, and have a high expectation of output. When you go in with a design thought through and tested, you come out with specific results.

The difference between a Compression Planning session and how most meetings are run is like the difference between a concert at Wolftrap and a high school band rehearsal when the director is home with the flu. Good facilitators always ask themselves, "How can we get the most creativity and highest level of thinking out of the group during the shortest time possible, and build all of it into a workable game plan?"

Use Compression Planning to Work on Collaborative Issues

The day is long gone when one person can walk into a room alone, figure something out, then come out and proclaim, "This is what I have decided. Go do it." It just doesn't work that way anymore – if it ever did. People want to be involved. They want understanding and clarity on an issue. But you can't string it out forever.

When a group of people get into something more than a casual conversation, they need a working structure. When you see eight people sitting around a table, all talking and one or several writing on notepads, you can bet they have eight different understandings of the same issue. They're not all working off the same premises, with the same set of assumptions. They don't have common reference points. They do not work well together. Compression Planning helps transform individuals into a group, and your group into a team.

 Use the Compression Planning System when you're trying to figure out where

you are and where you're going.

If your issue is something one person can't think through quickly by himself, crunch it out on a spreadsheet, or resolve it with a few phone calls, your issue is ripe for Compression Planning. If an engineer can design a solution with a CAD/CAM processor, you don't need a team.

Use Compression Planning to Build a Team

Often, in great frustration, a manager will say to me, "I don't care which way we go to market or which areas we attack to drive costs down. That's not crucial, maybe not even important. It is important, though, whatever we do, we do it together and that we get going now. We must be committed to getting there together."

This is the time for Compression Planning

If you have a choice of putting a team of eight people together for two days to resolve an issue or two days "to get to know, understand, and appreciate each other more," go for "resolving your issue" every time.

Bringing people together to handle problems or to move on opportunities encapsulates the essence of Compression Planning. A by-product of task and process together results in the formation of a team. Individuals come to understand, accept, and trust each other so they can be an effective team.

Compression Planning teams should be at the level of survivors in a life raft. A lot of meetings resemble cocktail party conversation. Our values come through in our work. Our beliefs permeate how we think and what we think about. That's where you engage people. When a group works to address an issue, they move towards being a high-performing team. Team-building is not a discrete activity. It's a by-product of the Compression Planning System. Your team grows out of the group's work together.

Use Compression Planning When Dealing with Complex Issues

Projects or issues that comprise a series of options, or several complex components that need to be rearranged, added to, or changed, require a process-oriented approach. Such was the case when publishers of the Scranton Times learned that their "friendly" competitor had been sold to an out-of-town communications giant. They organized a Compression Planning session to design a competitive response.

Addressing a complex issue such as this requires more than the simple transmission of information, as in "I tell you, you listen and come to insight." Your team needs to share information, digest, analyze, contribute ideas, and create concepts together. And they require continuous communication on a timely basis until you resolve your issue.

Compression Planning uses storyboards as its working medium to gather all data pertinent to your issue and displays it before your group. You capture ideas by printing them on cards and pinning them on your storyboards, thus giving your group continuous flexibility in developing ideas and building concepts. When we write personal notes, just talk, or record on flipcharts, your thinking seldom melds with what I'm thinking.

Use Compression Planning for Creativity and Innovation

In its elemental form, Compression Planning is creative planning done in a compression mode.

It is "creative" in the sense of bringing forth new ideas, insights, and fresh approaches, or just getting ideas out of people. Innovative products for introduction in an established market often begin this way. The process is "compressed" in the sense of squeezing excess time and extraneous influences out of team projects.

If you need to have creativity, to squeeze time out, to put disparate kinds of people together, or to just work together in a more interesting, fun, exciting, and high-energy way, then Compression Planning is your approach.

Use Compression Planning When the Issue Is "The Issue"

Sometimes your issue is to find "The Issue." Sometimes you know The Issue and you need to identify its parts. Sometimes you're not even sure what questions you should be asking.

Many times you are so close to a problem, so backed into a corner by it, you cannot make a clear statement of your issue. Chronic production problems often result from personal issues rather than mechanical failures. They suffer a pain level, a blockage, an obstruction obscuring your real issue, which could be political, financial, psychological, or even personal distractions.

Using storyboards to make an initial statement of your issue, to display background, and to raise questions often allows a team to clarify an issue. Once you achieve clarity, resolution of your issue is automatic or at least becomes a minor part of the task. But coming to clarity is difficult. People often say, "I didn't realize the true dimensions of my issue." The Compression Planning System will help get to an understanding of what you're really talking about. Then it's not uncommon to hear someone declare, "I didn't realize how many potential options I have related to this issue."

What the Mind Will Hold

Your mind can track seven items at one time, plus or minus two, according to memory experts. So when a spouse calls and says, "Honey, will you stop and get a dozen eggs, a can of Spam, Band-Aids, toothpaste, a gallon of milk, bread..."

A wise spouse always responds, "Wait, I'll write it down."

Now translate that common scene into the context of a meeting. Participants are handling multiple pieces of information, trying to sort out which comes first, second, and what lumps with what. Each person tries to fit facts into his own frame of reference while sorting out personal relationships and feeling pressure to get back to his "real job."

There has to be a better way. There is. In Compression Planning the pressure to remember is eliminated. With storyboards as your working medium, you capture all ideas and pin them in full view of your team. Concepts may be expanded, enhanced, organized, and reorganized at any time. With all of your facts displayed all the time, your group is free for "all-at-onceness" thinking about your issue and its resolution.

100 Issues for Compression Planning

THE TOPIC FOR THIS COMPRESSION PLANNING SESSION

1. Where are we in this business and where are we going?
2. What do we want from our principal suppliers?
3. What are the systems needs for a manufacturing unit?
4. What are the engineering design needs of the shipping department?
5. What are the options for dealing with a difficult executive team member?
6. Evaluate the need for a child-abuse hostel at the hospital.
7. Evaluate the advantages and drawbacks of going into business for myself after years with the same company.
8. Decide whether or not to set up a travel clearinghouse within this department.
9. Create unique approaches to get manufacturers to support trade association safety standards.
10. What are effective ways to keep senior management informed about what we're doing?
11. Identify five market targets for us in the federal government's program to rebuild the infrastructure.
12. Identify topics for a crucial presentation, with one hour to get ready.
13. Prioritize data processing needs.
14. Write a strategy to cut delinquent accounts 60 percent in 60 days.
15. Coordinate the work of Jerry McNellis and Jack Nettles in developing this book.

HOW TO...
16. Become absolutely indispensable to our customers.
17. Improve communication between plants in different cities.
18. Tap a new market in our industry.
19. Drive costs down in our business.
20. Start a day-care center at a work location.
21. Deal with a problem vendor we want to

keep.

22. Start a business selling Class A used cars.
23. Get employees to eat more healthful foods.
24. Get employees to stop smoking in your work area.
25. Retain people forced to work the second shift.
26. Double sales of a declining product line.
27. Cut mortgage application and approval time by 70 percent.
28. Provide publicity and recognition for the project implementation team.
29. Decrease customer complaints by 50 percent in three months.
30. Help a 12-year-old adjust to a new location when his parent is transferred to a new job.
31. Double membership of the association in 18 months.
32. Use the company's 75th anniversary to increase participation in the savings plan.
33. Get veteran employees to use all the software available to them.
34. Increase by 30 percent in six months the number of calls handled by 11 telemarketing representatives.
35. Help our family adjust to our move to another state.
36. Improve customer contacts by our agents.
37. Ensure 100 percent "voluntary." participation in the telephone courtesy training session.
38. Get long-term employees to accept and benefit from high-tech training.
39. Reduce paperwork 50 percent throughout the division.
40. Build the most loyal customer base in our industry.
41. Increase the % of time we spend with our major clients.
42. Raise $240,000 for my not-for-profit organization in six months.
43. Improve telephone coverage in our office.
44. Get technical experts to share their knowledge and skills with line personnel.
45. Cut recruiting costs by 20 percent.
46. Sell a $47,000 powerboat without a broker.
47. Turn around the "No" vote on the school bond issue.
48. Make the dealer marketing association better serve its members.
49. Significantly shorten the selection process for filling open positions.
50. Produce one year's worth of publications in six months.
51. Eliminate "pits" problem in lenses.
52. Build a service display booth for next year's announcement show with no budget.
53. Increase information-security awareness.
54. Wipe out drugs in the plant without infringing on employees' personal rights.
55. Settle a feud between supervisors in two departments.

WAYS TO...
56. Improve relations between doctors and the hospital staff.
57. Increase the number of job listings from alumni.
58. Resuscitate a food boutique that is just breaking even.
59. Reduce plant absenteeism quickly.
60. Create a mentor program for new employees of a large bank.
61. Call a union-management meeting to reorganize the maintenance department without provoking a wildcat strike.
62. Hold a workshop for oncology nurses to help them cope with problems in dealing with families of terminal patients.

63. Create a savings plan for my children's future.
64. Create a strategy to increase sales by 30 percent for a commercial photographer.
65. Create a benchmark program for an appliance manufacturer.

TO GENERATE...
66. Ideas for promoting free flu shots in the community.
67. Ideas for better packaging of a personal deodorant product.
68. Ideas for recognition awards for quality-improvement teams.
69. Five incredible concepts we can test for promoting light truck sales.

TO DEVELOP...
70. A plan to set up a weight-control group at work.
71. Strategies to get buyers to prefer American-built cars.
72. Ways to coordinate maintenance and operations scheduling.
73. A program to increase home ownership by low-income families.
74. An exercise program to meet mandated state requirements.
75. Three new products based on our _____0 technology.
76. Unique approaches for a week-long staff training program.
77. A master plan for installing the new production line.
78. Ways to improve teamwork between manufacturing and design when the two are 250 miles apart.
79. A "service" attitude among employees of this department.
80. A stress-management training program for 2500 employees.

81. A training program in our Mexico facility.
82. A marketing plan to double the size of our business over the next three years.
83. A master plan for relocating our offices.

TO DEVISE...
84. An in-house program to upgrade the technician's role in dealing with customers.
85. A strategy to increase a new hotel's market share by 30 percent in nine months.
86. A win-win strategy for labor/management negotiations.
87. A reward system for outstanding performance in the customer service division.

TO WRITE...
88. An orientation program to get new employees up to speed in three weeks.
89. A plan to do basic training on appliances, now that we no longer have a training center.
90. A plan to recruit volunteers within the agency for a telethon of stars.
91. A strategy for an insurer of health services to acquire and retain a target hospital as its customer.

TO PLAN...
92. The 25th annual meeting of the Engineering Society to attract 250 participants.
93. An open house for employees, families, and the community.
94. A funeral for a prominent person.

TO IDENTIFY...
95. Sites for 35 new convenience stores that will be profitable in 12 months.
96. More storage space for the property

department.
97. Ways to get more alums to help our college graduates land jobs.
98. A sure-fire way to get our product on the "Today Show."
99. The best giveaway item for a product promotion.
100. Solutions for shipping problems related to the return of damaged goods.

Chapter 4: The Planning Specialist

Compression Planning specialists have two principal functions. First, work with your client to design the team planning sessions. Second, facilitate your group meetings.

Chapter 10 covers Design, the most important fundamental of leading effective group meetings. In this chapter we explore the role of Compression Planning specialists as facilitators.

Think of an iceberg. Most of us remember, from third grade or the movie Titanic, that only a small part of an iceberg shows above the waterline. Most of it resides underwater. The iceberg serves as a useful model for what goes on in a planning session or any group endeavor. My good friend, psychologist Kendall Cowing, observed 20 percent of the substance of any meeting is content – the information, ideas, concepts related to the issue. Eighty percent of the substance is process – how the team works the content.

Content/Process Iceberg

Now think back to some of the groups you have worked with. If they resemble most groups, everybody focuses on content. Rarely is anybody concerned with how your group processes content.

In your typical business meeting, a boss assembles the troops and directs the proceedings. There is no question the boss is in charge. And why not; she is normally senior in age and length of service, has the biggest office, and makes the most money. Because she brings much content to the group and has a large stake in the outcome, the boss frequently struggles to focus on process. Still she assumes responsibility for how the meeting proceeds.

Sound familiar? Stir up any resentment?

I remember facilitating one stressful and exhausting session. After two days the issue was resolved. The team reached a tight consensus and everyone was committed to the game plan. When the head man asked how I felt working with his people, I paused for a long time before answering. It seemed like two minutes. At first, people laughed nervously as they waited for my answer; then they were silent. Finally I said, "At times I felt like a traffic cop at a kamikaze convention. I'm glad it all worked out."

In truth, without a neutral facilitator to look after the process and protect the players, the landscape would have been littered with dead ideas and bloody egos.

Focus on Process

Your role as a facilitator is to pay strict attention to process. If your issue is a sensitive one, you must be aware of the nuances of meaning and feelings. If your purpose is to be creative, you must encourage the sharing of all ideas while protecting the individuals who launch them.

Your role as a facilitator in the session will be affected by your stake in the issue and your position in the organization. On one extreme is the professional facilitator who is detached from content. At the other extreme is the in-house facilitator who participates in the content. In the latter case, other participants must help "keep the facilitator honest" so she can guide the process and still participate in the content. The relationship between content and process is insidious. Content tends to snatch you away from process. Even the best-intentioned facilitator can get wrapped up in content and forget the ground rules of the process. Most facilitators, with experience in facilitating and support from the planning team, learn to avoid the trap.

The Conductor as Model

I've found a good model for a Compression Planning specialist in the role of facilitator is an orchestra conductor. The conductor has studied the music score and the facilitator has created the design. The conductor gets things started, watches the rhythm of the group, keeps things moving, and signals players when to speed up, slow down, play softer, or come on forte. The facilitator fills a similar role, concentrating on process, supporting and encouraging some players, and restraining others, always centered on the purpose of the session.

Participants in a group are much like players in an orchestra – the cellist, percussionist, violinist, and bassoonist. The conductor wants to get a symphony out of those folks. She can't let the trumpet drown out everybody else. The piccolo player could be a shy, retiring person. The conductor must make sure the piccolo's music blends with sounds from the trumpet and the cello.

Conducting displays a wonderful mix of skill and art. The objective is music and conducting styles vary. Look at Paul Shaffer on the "David Letterman Show." He is a keyboard player and vocalist in the band, and also its director. There are infinite styles and roles...different styles, but each conductor helps his group make orchestral music.

Facilitators also develop individual styles. When you are in your role, remember no matter what your style, your objective is to enable your group to think and act at their creative best.

Characteristics of an Effective Facilitator

While facilitators' styles may vary, I do find certain characteristics common to most. The following are ones I have noted most often:

- Your number one skill as a facilitator is the ability to disengage. As a facilitator, you must not get so wrapped up in content you cannot manage the process. This is both a skill and a discipline.
- As a successful facilitator, you must be a good listener, talk in moderation, and be careful not to superimpose your values on the thoughts of others.
- Effective facilitators are mentally quick. You listen well and key off your group and the material.
- You can see patterns and trends in data. When looking at 50 ideas, facilitators have the skills to discern the five or six categories into which the ideas fall.
- Facilitators are people sensitive. You read subtle signs and sense shifts in the mood of your group and individuals.
- Effective facilitators hear not only ideas but also the principles behind the ideas. You burrow into a thought to extract the kernel, knowing the essence lies below the surface.

- You must be able to tolerate ambiguity and have the patience to work through complex issues resisting clear definition. The most effective facilitator is a centered person: you know what you are and what you are not. You know your strengths and your weaknesses. You try not to live your life for somebody else. Your life revolves around your own beliefs, codes, and creeds and you don't try to force those on other people.
- Skilled facilitators are outgoing, gentle, dynamic, or firm depending on which qualities are required at the moment. Your external response comes out of an internal balance and harmony. You are secure in yourself and can be "invisible" when needed to help your group.
- A facilitator protects ideas and egos. You are a good "conductor." You help the "flute" to play at its point in the score. That means holding off and toning down the trumpets, the cellos, or whatever else would drown out the flute, to allow the flute to make its music, its contribution.

People who are always turned ON usually make poor facilitators, because not all content lends itself to an ON approach. When I helped facilitate the board from the National Sudden Infant Death Syndrome Foundation, they worked with high anxiety at peak energy. They experienced some gentle, tearful times, but there were no turned ON times.

A so-so facilitator with a great design will do well. A great facilitator with a bad design will be lucky if the group can work through to closure.

Your Role as a Facilitator Is to:
- Develop the design for your session.
- Understand what is required to end with an action plan.
- Watch the timing and flow of the process and keep it moving.
- Be sensitive to energy levels of participants and your group as a whole.
- Protect the integrity and egos of individual participants.
- Keep the purpose and content of your session in mind while watching the process.
- Never have such a large stake in your issue you cannot manage the process. If you sense too much involvement, ask other participants to help keep you out of the content and help with the process.

At a boys' soccer game one evening, I watched as one of the players ran out of bounds into a piece of equipment and hurt himself. Somebody should have been watching the sidelines. The referee? The coach? That should have been decided before the game began. But no one was watching and the child was hurt. In group planning, keeping your players in-bounds and eliminating hazards to them is your job as the facilitator.

Manipulation Is Nonproductive and Destructive

The Compression Planning System is undone when someone tries to manipulate others into accepting a conclusion she has already reached. If your client has a plan in mind, you as the facilitator must bring it out and say to your group, "Let's work off this plan." That's honest. Your group may or may not settle for the original plan but, in the end, no one should feel left out or manipulated.

The facilitator's role keeps the group focused so it can search for and arrive at the truth. This is a delicate though vital role for the facilitator.

Ideas and Egos

Every idea has an ego attached to it. When somebody works up her courage and puts an idea before a group, she exposes her innermost thoughts and risks damage to her ego. Our sense of survival is so high, we find individuals will protect themselves before all else – before the organization, before the corporation, before the team. Your role as the facilitator is to make sure no one who takes the risk of offering an idea to the group gets kicked in the ego.

An Institute participant described what goes on at many meetings as "idea skeet." In a typical meeting, he observed, participants lie in wait until somebody launches an idea, then everybody shoots holes in it. They blast away until all the weaknesses are exposed. You do it too much and the person pulls back to protect herself, withdraws, and may have nothing substantial to say for the rest of your meeting.

For most people, ideas embody their most personal, sacred, revelation of themselves. They don't want their teeth kicked in by some insensitive lout who hasn't learned to respect others' egos. Your job as the facilitator aids in surfacing ideas, dealing with them, and making sure people are listening, hearing each other, and respecting the group's thinking. Later, they can make choices, judgments, and selections from all the ideas and concepts.

When you protect an idea, you protect the person behind the idea. How many times is someone with the solution to a problem unwilling to offer her ideas to the group and risk being skewered? We'll never know. Yet, we all remember times when someone came on so strong everybody else was intimidated and the process shut down. Working in a team requires a sensitive, delicate balance of all personalities involved. Your role as a facilitator is to perceive these nuances and to help your team come to a resolution and develop plans or whatever they must accomplish with no casualties left in the field.

Don't Aim for a Perfect World

When working on a team project, shoot for 60 percent improvement. Don't aim for a perfect world. Regroup later and reach for more. My brother Jim McNellis refers to this as "gentle migration." That's how you get things done. Many people aim for a perfect world and nothing happens. They study a problem forever rather than accept incremental movements forward to see what they can learn that will move them to the next step.

When we started writing this book, Jack Nettles and I knew close to nothing about writing books. We know more now than we did because we started moving on it. If we had aimed for the perfect book our first time, we would have been frustrated to inaction.

Focus on Process

The last time I went to the circus, I found myself watching the ground crew instead of the acts. They sure were harmonized, and were synchronized like the performers. They had to be to get all the rigging and props in place. Crewmembers ran from one ring to another. They jumped over cables. They hauled equipment into the air and locked it in place. They watched from behind the scenes, so those up front could perform for the paying customers.

As a facilitator, you take on the role of the ground crew for a planning group. Details such as light, heat, air conditioning, food, timing, setting, and the mood...you need to pay attention to all of these details. If these details are right, your group can process content. If they're not, the "performers" run in all directions, stumble over each other, and accomplish little. What contaminates a referee right away? Being for one side or the other. The same goes for facilitators. Don't get too involved in content. Stick with process.

The Principle of Elegance

A lot of people try to do too many things, too big, too much at once. The principle of elegance says do a few things so well they radiate into other things.

To be elegant is to be simple, refined, polished, outstanding, choice, splendid, superb, superior, clean...aaah, to be elegant. Yes, and Compression Planning can help you achieve that elegance. You can generate many ideas and plans in Compression Planning, many more than you will need. The drive for elegance is to decide what you will do and what you will not do. This combination brings focus. Combine, simplify, and sort, and then you will achieve elegance.

Pick three or four key actions, then pull them off to energize your attention and focus on those manageable three or four. This way, you are not trying to figure out what to do with 40 things that are impossible to manage and ultimately just won't get done. Such failure can only foster doubt, cynicism, and disappointment in the team.

Intuition

Life wouldn't go on without intuition. Your doctor intuitively arrives at a diagnosis. The more experience she has, the more intuitive she proves to be. Good doctors use all of their diagnostic and analytic skills, and their intuition. Facilitators also rely on their skills, plus a full measure of intuition. This comes back to the concept of centeredness, which means being in touch with yourself – what you know, what you have experienced, what you deduce, what you feel. People with intuitive skills don't always know how to articulate what they sense. Unfortunate others don't know it is okay to be intuitive.

Chapter 5: The Centered Life Of An Outside Facilitator

I don't believe it's possible to effectively facilitate outside your personal values. For example, I would not facilitate for a company selling cigarettes. Nor would I facilitate with an organization whose primary purpose is to do abortions. Those represent my values. They may not be yours, but they are mine. I cannot serve in a facilitation role for something violating my personal values.

Degree of Difficulty

No facilitator should undertake projects beyond his capability to handle, are above his head, or are outside his scope. New facilitators are particularly vulnerable to someone else's insistence and their own desire to help.

Successes and Failures

As an outside facilitator, you accept even though you may work with a team on a project, the ultimate success or failure of a project is theirs and their successes are their successes. You may share their pride, but the credit for success is theirs. Nor are you to take the blame as facilitator when they miss the mark. Their failures also are their failures. You do your best and move on.

Appropriateness

People have a tendency to fall in love with Compression Planning. Being enamored gets in your way of serving people because facilitators, particularly those who have newly discovered its potential, want to tackle all issues for all people in all circumstances. Use the process where appropriate to help your client.

And remember, a facilitator never stops watching the process. Facilitators are not on stage. You may be up front, but you often need to be invisible while other participants take the lead.

When facilitating at my most effective level, I am comfortable with myself and the process to the degree it allows me to be thoroughly comfortable working with you. Then when I am doing things, I am doing them for your sake rather than for my own kicks.

My friend and mentor, psychologist Ken Cowing, told me you should not put more energy into the session than your client. Ineffective facilitation goes on when you work harder than the people you serve. If they are not involved and committed to resolving the issue, the outcome will be limited at best.

Time

Being realistic about time demands is a slice of honesty. I believe taking on a task when your client will not give you enough time for legitimate things to happen is unprofessional. Giving you two hours to figure out a problem he has been wrestling with for 20 years is absurd. The centered facilitator has to say, "I don't know how to do that." The uncentered person may say, "Hey, I've got a chance to help do something and be a star," and serve neither the client nor himself well.

I encourage people to remain a student facilitator for life. Do it and you will grow beyond belief in effectiveness. A centered person will point to the middle of a curve and say, "I'm here on the learning curve." He will not try to pass himself off as any higher or any lower. Centered people are in touch with where they are.

On Centering the Person

An interesting little book to guide you as a

facilitator, an effective leader of groups, and coach of others, is *The Tao of Leadership* by John Heider, Bantam Books. I can see how some people will take issue with parts of this new age philosophy. Perhaps I do too, but listen to these paragraphs from the book:

- "The well run group is not a battlefield of egos. Of course there will be conflict, but these energies become creative forces."

- "If the leader loses sight of how things happen, quarrels and fear devastate the group field."

- "This is a matter of attitude. There is nothing to win or lose in group work. Making a point does not shed light on what is happening. Wanting to be right blinds people."

- "The wise leader knows that it is far more important to be content with what is actually happening than to get upset over what might be happening but isn't."

Heider's book is a resource to trigger thoughts to help a person get centered whether he is a member of the group or the "servant" of the group. The servant of a Compression Planning group, in Heider's sense, is the neutral facilitator. When I am there as a professional facilitator, I am there only to serve the needs of the group. When I am the facilitator and a participant, I am a servant/participant. When I am the client, I need a strong facilitator who will free me to be an effective participant.

The role of facilitator is not a natural pursuit for most people. To be effective requires skill that can be learned, such as sensitivity, which must be nurtured, and intuition, which should be trusted. These and the qualities described above are substance for the regimen of a healthy facilitator.

Chapter 6: Selecting And Recruiting Your Team

Selecting the right participants is key to effective Compression Planning, just as recruiting talented musicians is indispensable to a splendid concert. If you need a potent plan, choose a potent team.

Compression Planning teams form from either natural or disparate groups.

Natural groups have an established relationship. They may be the senior staff of a corporation, the crew and supervisors in a production center, or the trauma team in a hospital. A board of directors is a natural group, as is a family planning their vacation. You don't have a choice who will be included in a natural group. If you exclude any natural member of the group, you may diminish the long-term effectiveness of your team.

Natural groups can be effective, especially after they have worked through several challenging issues. Teams skilled in Compression Planning can do in hours or a day what many groups do in weeks or months. They are good because they have incredible respect for each other. They listen intently to the words and principles when others speak. They focus 100 percent on the issue. Such seasoned teams could be a model for any business.

Disparate groups usually address specific issues or devise strategies to handle unique opportunities. You might put together such a team to design your factory of the future, plan a key customer meeting, or craft a marketing strategy. Each person is selected for what he or she contributes in the way of knowledge, skills, or position.

A primary metals company, hoping to tap into the road and bridge market as the U.S. rebuilds its infrastructure, recruited a unique group of individuals to examine the possibilities. In addition to the company's own market development people, the project team included a truck driver, a state trooper, a government planner, a homemaker, a professional futurist, and a construction company owner. In one day they targeted six products with high potential, assigned teams to investigate, and wrote a plan for arriving at go/no-go decisions on them.

Compression Planning works equally well with natural groups or disparate teams. In my experience, numerous problems happen in natural groups when you can't exclude people who have little to contribute. In practice, you almost always have the option to add selected participants if they can be expected to strengthen your team.

Even if you design and facilitate for your chief executive officer and her vice-presidents, you should ask: Who else needs to be included? Who could we involve to make this a richer mix, get a broader view, a different perspective? Keep in mind, however, you want your session to be workable and productive. Although useful, adding an outsider to a natural group can be an intrusion, so weigh the risk carefully.

There's a kind of upward pressure to include everyone who might have an interest in your issue and a downward pressure to keep your group lean and within the function. As a rule of thumb, keep your number of participants to a maximum of 12, and make sure you have a diverse group.

When working through a project involving several departments or production centers, include somebody upstream and somebody down-stream in the production flow. If you have only participants in the "middle of your mess," they tend to point fingers: "Well, if the users would do this..." or "If only our vendors would do..." Build your team so when decisions are made, they can also be implemented by the team's authority. That's the ideal.

Team Size and Composition

Select and recruit members of your team as carefully as you design the work they will do. Here are key guidelines.

Your ideal size for a planning team is five to seven people, although 10 to 12 is workable. This number of people can gather comfortably around a table to work with the storyboarding materials. They can hear and see each other and easily read the storyboards. The facilitator can keep up with the action and ensure everyone can contribute and be heard.

Large groups work when led by a team of skilled facilitators. The technique is to repeatedly break a large group into smaller working units and merge their output. Planning with large groups should be avoided unless there are compelling reasons for doing so.

Spectators should not be allowed in a Compression Planning session. Someone who says, "I'll just sit in the back of the room and watch," will inhibit your group. A boss lurking around the perimeter will do a disservice to your group and to herself. Either you participate or you are out. "Secretaries" are seldom employed to take notes. Have your group members print their ideas on cards and pin them on the storyboards.

High-performing teams comprise a variety of participants. Even when selecting a natural team, strive for a mixture that includes:

- Various levels in the organization. These add strength. Don't be afraid to mix senior management with technicians, production workers, and office personnel. If everyone follows the guidelines, your mix can be dynamite. Everyone has something to contribute, and they bring different perspectives to the issue.

- Include male, female, young, and older, employees and customers.

- Experts who know your topic in detail, co-perts who know about the topic, in-perts who bring a fresh view or naiveté by asking: Why? How? What if?

- At least one "numbers person."

- A free spirit to shake up tight minds.

- "A friend of the court" who has access to the mighty because he has earned their respect.

- Free consultants such as friends, customers, bankers, and vendors.

- A mix of personality and social styles.

Most meetings are ineffective because they go on without ground rules for the participants and without any thought regarding how to proceed when the group gets together. Compression Planning works because it has ground rules, a design for your session, and a neutral facilitator to lead the process.

Working in a compression mode requires a behavioral change for many people. It is easy to learn, but change is essential. Experienced participants delay judgment, don't talk too much, speak to the point, enhance each other's ideas, and seldom lock down too soon on ideas.

Recruiting Your Planning Team
Recruiting is always most effective when done face to face.

1. State your expectations for the session. Share with each participant your purpose and non-purpose of the session and key questions to be addressed. Explain that you will introduce a method of working together that may be new for them.

2. Don't oversell the process. Just set the tone and your expectations for the session. Tell them, for example, "We will meet for three hours and walk out with eight to ten ideas to help tighten our cash flow over the next 120 days. Two or three of those ideas will be implemented within five days."

3. Recruit people to your design. Share with them the background, overall purpose of your project, purpose and non-purpose of the session, and the key questions they will be addressing.

4. For first-time users of Compression Planning, don't be afraid to say, "I'm trying this new process for looking at

problems and planning action. Will you help me try it out?" Stay in a learning mode. Don't set yourself up as an expert. Don't set the process up as the fad of the month.

5. Orient people to the process and explain they will learn how the system works and how to begin using it themselves.

A good-looking storyboard with a clean design builds confidence and excitement. People want to be confident you know what you are doing. Start with simple tasks so you can navigate the storyboard easily and generate good ideas. Then, with some experience under your belt, move on to more complex tasks. You will be more confident and comfortable with the Compression Planning System as you begin to tackle major projects.

6. Tell them why they have been chosen and who else will be in your group. If someone is an expert, a co-pert, or an in-pert, let her know why she is included. Tell them how you set up your project team.

Someone is sure to say, "I don't know much about this issue." You counter with, "But you're a good thinker. We need fresh ideas and I'm counting on you." Clients and customers are often are in a unique position to help with projects. At the suggestion a client be included on the team, a corporate-type may object, "Oh no. We can't hang out our dirty linen for her." The truth is our clients see our mistakes before we do, and they can help with the solutions. It's a rare client who doesn't feel complimented when asked to help think through critical issues in which he has a stake. Often, clients feel freer to give you ideas than others closer to your problem.

Invest time answering questions for participants and making them comfortable, to generate positive energy for the experience. If people arrive angry because "I've been roped into wasting time in another meeting," you have a lot of resistance to overcome. If people arrive eager to help and believe you know what you're doing, they will make contributions far beyond your expectations.

Groups Where Diversity Has Helped

An unusual strategic session for the executive director of a medical society netted valuable side benefits in working relationships. To develop a five-year plan for the organization, he assembled the society directors, officers, and staff, about 18 people, for a day-and-a-half of Compression Planning. The staff had never participated with the directors on a project. The group wrote the five-year plan, and, in the process, built a team committed to the plan, and committed to each other.

A new director who attended his first meeting of the board was amazed. "In a short time," he said, "I learned more about this organization and feel more a part of it than any board I have ever served on."

The essence of his new experience was nobody told him what was expected of him and his role became obvious. In this shared experience with key people, he learned about the organization and became a part of it. Most groups would have brought in the new director to walk through the by-laws and halls, shake a few hands, show and tell, march and burp.

Hasn't Everybody Had This Problem?

The director of training for a pharmaceutical company – over several months – spent, "ten minutes here, five minutes there," complaining, looking through catalogs, talking to friends, thinking about it in "the shower", while searching for a special memento to mark the end of a training session.

Most people in business have boxloads of these things. You get one and either throw it out or, if you're into guilt, you stash it on a shelf in your garage. Our man wanted something so special participants would display it for their friends and reinforce the lessons they had learned.

Typically, what would you do? Go down the hall, grab a few people and ask them to help you think this through, right? Right! He had tried that. Several times. It didn't work.

After learning about Compression Planning, he decided to give it one more shot, and he recruited a team of people who knew nothing about the program. The group included a financial guy, a systems person, an organizational development-type, and a communications specialist.

Working in a Compression Planning mode, he gave a brief description of the problem and set his expectations: "In an hour I want to walk out with three unique concepts I can prototype, get costs on, and hire a vendor to make. Three sensational ideas! Help me."

They creamed it with three super ideas! One of the ideas he chose was to hire an artist to draw a caricature of everybody at the seminar and present them at the last session.

This may not be brain surgery, but hasn't everybody had to deal with a variation on this problem? Such is the reality of organization life.

Breaking Down Barriers

Many corporations using the Compression Planning approach combine different levels and layers in their planning teams. You can take marketing-types, engineers, accountants, and production workers and mix them up, slice across and up and down your organization, to get a rich broth in which to nurture creative solutions to old problems.

One of the most creative organizations we know commissions groups including members of the board, operating personnel, and other positions throughout the company. Corporate officers and staff travel to operating locations where they involve local people in addressing issues with corporate significance. They combine lab directors, operators, transportation, marketing, and salespeople who otherwise seldom have the opportunity to talk with each other.

The dynamic tension diversity sets up is fascinating and productive. These are clear thinkers. They are bright, though not overly articulate people. The tendency in most organizations, unfortunately, is to still have human resource people talk with their own, engineers with engineers, bosses with bosses. No wonder they keep getting the same old answers to the same old questions. Diversity builds effective groups that wring fresh opportunities from old problems.

Size of Your Group

Although five to seven is your ideal size for a group, in practice groups range from two to several dozen. The following formula gives insight into why small groups are more effective for team planning.

The number of relationships in any group can be calculated this way:

$$(N \times [N - 1]) / 2 = \text{Number of Relationships and Interconnections}$$

"N" represents the total number of people in your group.

Increase the number of people in your group to seven and fill in the formula:

$$(7 \times [7\text{-}1]) / 2 = 21$$

Now you have 21 connections to be made in listening, hearing and sensing, tuning into, and tuning out. Raise your group size to 15 and you have created 105 connections. By now you begin to see the complexity of working with larger groups. The number of connections gets to be astronomical. Everybody can't hear or see everybody else. How can they listen or pay attention to each other? You get side conversations. People track off on their own. The group loses its effectiveness.

Large groups can be broken down into small teams to simultaneously work on the same topic or on different aspects of the same topic. The teams then reassemble as a large group and join their ideas to create an action plan. This process is called "synergistic convergence."

Role of the Participant

My good friend Dr. Trevor Macpherson once asked me, "Do you know why Molly Dapena is such a good leader?" His answer: "Because she excels as a participant. When she takes a turn as facilitator, the others use her as their model for what a participant should be." When Dr. Dapena is the leader, she encourages, supports and helps her participants. When she participates, she encourages, supports, and helps the leader. What do you think the participants want to do when she stands up to lead? They want to help her be successful.

Every member of a Compression Planning team has a responsibility to stay within the rules of collaborative work and help others do the same. To be responsible is to work with the process as well as the content. So, remember:

- Explore ideas (your own and others' as well).
- Be tolerant of ambiguity.
- Practice the art of building on others' ideas.
- Stay engaged until the work is done.
- Avoid locking down on an idea too soon.

When we talk about a facilitator in Compression Planning, we are speaking of the servant leader. This is the role of helping others to be effective. It is not "the boss" who tells everybody what to do and how to do it. The servant leader draws ideas out and protects the egos attached to them.

This works off the theory people have within themselves the answers to their own questions. The servant leader helps them discover what they know – or to reach the point where they know what they don't know. When new knowledge comes, they are ready to make use of it.

An important role for the facilitator is to teach participants to be participants and let them learn by doing. That is why you debrief after every session, asking your team "What went right?" and, "What could be done better next time?" Using the process often helps an organization develop experienced, seasoned participants.

Every Compression Planning session has a purpose and ends with a plan to move the project forward. This may sound contrived, but it's not. Expectations and results are different when the leader suggests, "We are here to talk about..." than when she says, "The purpose of this session is to walk away with specific answers and a plan of action."

Chapter 7: Essentials For A Team Workplace

Compression Planning is a spirited activity. Participants get involved physically as well as mentally. They need space for a table, chairs, and storyboards. And room to move about.

More and more organizations, recognizing the importance of team projects, set aside special rooms for this purpose. Teams can walk into a well-equipped space any time, shut the door, and be isolated to do their work. Commercial conference centers and hotel meeting areas have responded to this mode of working, but few are equipped to handle storyboarding.

Your objective is to provide an environment in which project teams can be what our colleague Nan Foltz calls "fully present." Without distractions, teams can focus 100 percent on an issue until they have constructed concepts and committed to a plan of action. If your project continues for several weeks or months, as with many development programs, a team room may stay set for the duration of your work.

The environment needed for Compression Planning remains the same whether it occurs at your own location or off-site. Your location may have the advantage of having a well-equipped, dedicated space and is always ready to go. The drawback to working on-site is business people on their own turf are too available. Their focus differs when only a door separates them from colleagues, subordinates, and the boss.

High-powered strategic thinking should be held off-site, at least an hour away by car or plane, depending on your group. Unless you are far enough away, participants go to the office before and after your session, and even during lunch, trying to do "my job" instead of concentrating on the planning session when their real job is planning the future of the enterprise.

Knowing no one can be summoned for a "quick conference" allows your group to focus all its energy on your project and to stay on target for the agreed-on length of time. When your purpose is "to write a three-year plan for doubling revenues and increasing profits by 200 percent," you can't afford to have your people check out early, mentally or physically.

Logistics are more difficult when you work out of town. When you do go off-site, be thorough with the logistics and be ready for surprises. Anticipate materials may be lost and planes may arrive late. That way you won't be undone. With studious planning and determination, off-site locations can be made to work well.

You can read a special "White Paper" I wrote on off-site retreats by going to www.compressionplanning.com.

Working with Conference Center Staff

The Compression Planning System is beyond the experience of most hotels and conference centers. It incorporates many elements of conventional planning approaches, but the differences require special equipment, a flexible staff, and diligent attention to detail on your part.

When you make arrangements for your off-site location, identify one conference center employee by name to be your primary contact. This is someone you can go to when all else fails or you need a special service. Arrive early and spend time with this person. Study the layout of the whole facility. Check out your planning rooms and get them set to your satisfaction.

Identify by name the service person in charge of setting and resetting rooms. If you need to work in the evenings, find out who manages the second shift. Write down the phone number you can call to reach these people at any time. When service people do a good job, recognize their efforts with words and money.

The most perceptive and effective conference center manager I have ever known is Gary Armitage. He is devoted to the principle of "learning and planning is optimized in a distraction-free environment," and he asks, "Why else would anybody willingly leave the office to attend a conference?" Gary's shorthand way of promising an effective team workplace: "You won't be in the middle of a meeting on downsizing your company while a wedding is going on behind the next partition."

Be Specific When Reserving your Space

Reserve your meeting rooms 24-hours a day during the period you will be using them. Ask for the same rooms throughout your session. Arrange to set up the night before your first meeting if possible. Avoid having to break down your rooms for evening functions so you don't have to remove your storyboards or, worse, strip the material from your boards. The staff never gets your arrangement back exactly the way you want it. Resetting your rooms yourself will drain energy and add to your frustration.

Meeting Rooms

Few hotels and conference centers have had experience accommodating groups using story-boards as their working medium. They're accustomed to using PowerPoint, grease boards, flip charts, and computers. They will not know how to set up your tables, chairs, storyboards, and materials table. Pay particular attention to easels. They must be sturdy enough to hold your storyboards securely while your group works with them. We once had a fragile easel tip over and start a chain reaction, bringing 10 easels and boards crashing down. This problem is so pervasive we work with a company (storyboardtools.com) that ships easels, storyboards, and storyboarding supplies for sessions we lead. They also rent easels and storyboards to our clients.

Few meeting planners or conference center staff will believe the amount of space groups need to move about in the planning area. You must insist. Send detailed instructions, including room dimensions. A sketch of your meeting room layout with an overhead view of your planning room is helpful but it won't guarantee the space you need, so arrive early. Be prepared to reset your rooms and to insist on larger accommodations if they are cramped. Check to see if your staff is unionized. I almost shut down an entire New York hotel when I rearranged a meeting room by myself.

For many of your larger sessions, the ideal size is close to 1,600 to 2,400 square feet. This provides adequate space for your team to work as a whole and for smaller groups to break out. You will need tables to hold extra supplies and snack foods.

List of materials used in Compression Planning

Larger groups will, of course, need larger

spaces. You must insist! We have facilitated groups so large they occupied a hotel ballroom and breakout rooms as well. The largest space we have ever used was the immense exhibition hall of the Ohio State Fairgrounds. An area was set for 165 people to work as a group. Small planning centers to accommodate four to five people were set in the same room and in several breakout areas.

It is easiest to keep your team in one area, with separate planning areas in your room to handle the required number of small groups. When more than two groups work in one area, their talk becomes background noise, masking the separate group activity. In practice, we often do not have ideal accommodations so we adapt to what is available.

With bigger groups, use different rooms for each subgroup of six to ten people to insulate your groups from each other's noise. Be sure to check out room sizes and locations. Insist on rooms located near your large meeting area. Otherwise, you will use a lot of energy traveling back and forth between floors or down long halls. Test the temperature controls in every room.

More About Noise

Noise can be a big problem. At an Ivy League college, we were overcome by the traffic noise coming through the windows and the roar of fans set up to overcome the lack of air conditioning. Our only choice was to shout and make the best of a bad situation. In another location, we battled the noise of jackhammers and wailing alarms as the hotel staff tested its new fire alarm system. When we explained the problem, the hotel management rescheduled further fire alarm tests and moved the jackhammers to another area of the remodeling project while we worked.

You should do everything possible to avoid such "disasters." If you can, examine your meeting area and its surroundings before you book your space. Otherwise, get someone in the area to check it out. Ask lots of questions. Be sure to inquire about events scheduled for adjacent rooms. If you are not satisfied, tell the staff. If they cannot solve your problem, look for another conference center.

When your group assembles for the first time, be sensitive to physical impairments of individuals. Look for hearing aids, which are much more common than they used to be, especially among men. If you spot someone having trouble hearing, ask if he wants to move up front, then watch to see if he can hear what you say. Background noise from forced air heating and cooling systems can be troublesome.

If you want a free copy of our current checklist and room setup diagrams, call 724.847.2120 or go to www.compressionplanning.com.

Heating, Cooling, and Public Address

At least once during every session, somebody or everybody is going to be too hot or too cold. Locate the thermostat and learn how to adjust it. If you can't adjust it yourself, find out who can and write down the phone number. Ditto for piped-in music. Someone other than the facilitator should be in charge of the temperature and bothersome sounds.

Even though fewer people smoke today, I suggest you address the smoking issue head-on and early. Smokers are invited to call a break when they need to or they can leave the room when they want to smoke. You seldom have a problem with smoking when you establish guidelines upfront.

Only with groups of 50 or more in cavernous rooms should you use public address systems. First try to raise your voice a decibel or two. If needed, find out how to operate the system and ask the technician to stand by until you're sure it's working. A lavaliere or wireless microphone will give you the most freedom to move and work with your storyboards.

Materials You Ship to your Site

Ship early. Alert your conference location. Call ahead to check on arrival of your materials. Bring the telephone number and other information on your shipper. Find out who is in charge of receiving at your hotel and try to locate a local source for cards, pins, markers, and other materials in case yours don't arrive or you run short.

Tables and Chairs

For each planning area or breakout room, have a table large enough to accommodate all but one of your participants (you, the facilitator) on three sides. For a group of seven, a table measuring six feet on each side is comfortable. The facilitator stands on the side with the storyboards. One of your participants may also be asked to pin cards as your session revs up.

Chairs should be comfortable and light enough to be lifted or rolled easily.

Never agree to work in a hotel's showplace boardroom. Any space not filled by the ponderous table is gobbled up by the matching chairs that can hardly be moved without assistance. Usually, lighting is so "tasteful" you even have

trouble finding the obligatory antique samovar on the carved sideboard.

By the way, this is a samovar ...

... yes, an ornate coffee urn.

Lighting

Check out your lighting when you first arrive at an off-site location. Make sure all your fixtures have their full compliment of bulbs or fluorescent tubes. If any are missing or burned out, insist they be replaced. Find out where the light switch is located. Check it out. If lights are controlled by a rheostat, run it up to full power. Lighting in planning rooms should be bright. Low light levels drain energy and tend to be depressing. Daylight from windows is desirable if it isn't in the back of your storyboards and the facilitator. Looking into a bright window is quite uncomfortable. Participants should be able to read the cards without straining to see. Key lights on your storyboards help focus your group's attention.

I once checked out the lighting in a fancy executive conference room and told the client, "We must have more light on the storyboards when we meet next month." He called the building manager to take care of it. After three meetings with the engineers, the building manager reported nothing could be done in time for the sessions. When my associate Pam Ellis arrived in the meeting room, she climbed onto a table and repositioned the reflectors in their fixtures to highlight the storyboards rather than the tables. Her get-it-done approach saved the day.

Transportation and Lodging

Someone on your planning team or the hotel staff should be designated to coordinate transportation for participants, especially for remote conference locations. Furnish participants with schedules for ground transportation, where to find limousines and rental cars, and clear road instructions. Offer to help. Near the end of your conference, remind everyone about check-out time and shuttle departure schedules. Ask if anyone needs assistance.

As for lodging, each participant should have a private room that is comfortable and quiet. Compression Planning is strenuous, so restful sleep is important. Group members may handle reservations directly with the conference center or through your office. Either way, be sure to brief your center on what to expect and how to handle reservations.

Meals and High-Energy Foods

If your group is small, participants can use the common eating facilities. We have found luncheon buffets work best. This compresses eating time and gives participants an opportunity for a walk before returning to work. If possible, have meals away from your meeting room for a change of scenery. This also gives the facilitator time to get ready for your next session. Menus should be planned to help maintain high energy.

In Compression Planning sessions, breaks are not scheduled according to usual custom. You take them as your work permits and for the purpose of reenergizing your group. Food and beverages should be available throughout the day and freshened by the hotel or conference center staff.

Watch out for treats from the chef. A chocolate swirl topped with cream for lunch will have half your group dozing by two o'clock. The staff at one location where we work serves popcorn mid-afternoon. The aroma of cooking popcorn floating through the meeting rooms is a mild distraction soon overcome by the taste and the lift from eating the hot popcorn.

Exercise

Lots of people are into regular exercise programs and request running trails, exercise machines, pools, and other workout facilities. Encourage mild exercise to help wind down at the end of the day and to reenergize after lunch or when your group has gone into a slump. I discourage competitions or strenuous exercise that drains energy, takes too much time, or proves to be a mental diversion.

Communications Support

Since you are looking for isolation and not exile, communications are important to the functioning of your planning sessions and for your individuals. Prohibit cell phones in your meeting rooms. Have the top person set the pace by turning off her phone in front of your group and asking everyone to do the same. Discourage messages from being delivered during your session.

Chapter 8: Storyboarding

All-at-Onceness Thinking

Most groups have a way to record what goes on in their working sessions. They write on flipcharts, someone takes notes, or the boss "remembers" and dictates a report. Many meetings, perhaps most, have no well-thought-out agenda or list of topics to discuss. Some make no pretense of recording what goes on. After all, they seem to reason, everybody hears the same things, has a chance to have a say, and they all agree on the conclusions. That's the way it's supposed to work and the way it's always been done. But test these assumptions.

Have you ever come away from a meeting wondering what actually happened, what was decided, and if anybody was going to do anything about it — whatever "it" turned out to be? Most people in business and organization life spend untold hours in meetings like this, and many of them tell us they are frustrated beyond endurance.

The Compression Planning System is the antithesis of this "sit, talk, and take notes" approach to leading groups. You design every compression session. You print your design in large, block letters on cards, and your cards are arranged on four-foot-square storyboards displayed in your meeting room. Everybody's ideas and concepts from that point forward are printed on cards and displayed on storyboards. This records and displays the total team thinking. We call this visual, interactive mode "all-at-onceness thinking."

With storyboards, your groups have a medium allowing them to see the whole of an issue at the same time they are working on its parts. Your boards display the past and present of your group's thinking while their future plans unfold.

Your objective, of course, is to compress the planning time and still give everybody an opportunity to contribute their ideas to the total thinking of your group.

The innovation in storyboarding lending itself to Compression Planning is the speed with which your group can work. Ideas and information on storyboards can be reorganized and restructured while your group continues to develop new ideas. Your team prints its own report with the cards, thus preventing premature filtering of ideas and speeding up your planning.

When your Stomach Keeps Score

Author John Powell has observed when emotions are unexpressed, your stomach keeps score. Admitting an issue exists — getting it out of your head, heart, and gut, getting it up on a storyboard and sharing it with other people — is a key step in its resolution.

Storyboarding won't allow you to avoid or deny an issue once you display it before your group. When people express their fears, needs, hopes, and plans on a storyboard, amazing forces are set in motion.

The mechanics of storyboarding are simple. Ideas are printed on cards of four sizes and colors to designate:

- Topic = Topic card (7" blue card)
- Major headings = Header cards (4" x 6" cards)
- Sub-headings = Subber cards (3" x 5" or 4" x 6" yellow card)
- Modifiers or expanders = Sider cards (2" x 3" green card)

A Fast, Flexible Way to Keep Score

Storyboarding provides a fast way of moving a group from talking about an issue to getting it where it can be seen and developed into rich ideas and clear, crisp concepts. You achieve those rich ideas and clear, crisp concepts by showing the cards, labeling colors and sizes. Show them on a board so they can be seen by all. Most people who use flipcharts are blown away by the speed of using storyboards as their working medium, especially when the time comes to sort and coalesce ideas into an action plan.

A typical storyboard carries 75 to 100 bits of information. You can see the interconnections and relationships of ideas, and you can change those instantly. The process is faster than a Mac with a mouse. You remove a card. Slide it over here. Move it there. If you're working on a grease board, you can't do this. How do you move an idea from left to right for clarity when your idea is written on a flipchart? With cards on a storyboard, you can move ideas or rearrange your entire concept. You can take ideas from one board to another. Storyboarding allows people to innovate while participating.

Everybody Participates

Compression Planning with storyboarding is fast paced. Everybody participates. Everybody takes turns at printing cards, pinning, and leading the group. I have been in sessions where people who couldn't speak were able to participate by printing their ideas on cards.

In another group, a team member could not write. He was a bright but functionally illiterate adult. By listening and following the action, he contributed ideas and took a turn at facilitating the group, which included some PhDs. No matter what their education level, participants seem to grasp the relationships, connections, flow, and development of ideas in the planning.

Walt Disney observed that people want to be involved, and he saw storyboarding as another way to get them into the process. Walk into a planning center using storyboards, and you can grasp what is going on. Even without understanding how the system works, you can participate. By reading the cards, you can get up to speed and start to participate without interrupting the pace. That's a huge benefit.

At most meetings, if someone arrives late, she struggles to understand what's going on. When everyone in your group takes turns printing cards, pinning, and leading, everybody gains intellectual and physical ownership of the project in a way they don't get from other meeting processes. Everybody takes on functional roles and helps to move the work along. This breaks through one of your biggest barriers to collaborative planning: the power-posturing between boss and subordinate, senior, and junior group members.

This approach also helps to hurdle your cultural barriers that occur when several nationalities are mixed on a team. One session I facilitated was comprised of Japanese, Korean, Chinese, Indonesian, and European participants. The American sponsors worried how things would go and so did the Europeans. They knew in most settings, because of their cultural backgrounds, Asians assume a super-polite, seemingly subservient role. Their intellect races ahead but their ideas are concealed to avoid offense.

The Asians were in their traditional character during the first day: polite and deferential. The Americans and Europeans seemed to plow them under. But during the second day, the scene was different. The cultural masks disappeared. Everybody joined the team on equal footing and the project moved along quickly. Compression Planning enabled that group to reach beyond their differences and to focus on finding solutions to their common interests.

Ground Rules Establish Order

Storyboarding is not just an exercise in printing on cards and sticking them on boards with pushpins. Groups operate within definite ground rules, even though sessions are active and sometimes loud.

Four simple rules guide your group during the exploration or creative thinking phase of a session:
- Suspend judgment for now.
- Listen to each other.
- Spin vague thoughts into rich ideas.
- Make no speeches – limit your contribution to 45 seconds or less.

A different set of four ground rules apply in your analytical phase of the process:
- Attack ideas, not people.
- Narrow down to a manageable few ideas.
- Focus on unique factors.
- Merge ideas to create strength.

Most groups welcome guidelines, knowing the absence of rules encourages chaos. Watch a sporting event and you get the point. What would a game be without a referee, and how would a referee function without rules? How would you know when to start a play, stop your game, or declare a winner? With rules and a referee, you can participate and give it your best without fear of being ground up by the other players.

Just think about what would happen in a football game if there were no sideline boundaries. In the huddle, the quarterback could say to the tight end, "You run up in the stands and I'll throw you the ball. They'll never tackle you there." Right!

In our sessions, we function within guidelines. The facilitator (referee) calls back players who drift into the stands. Experienced teams police themselves on a playing field made level by a few simple rules that help them be effective.

Chapter 9: Compression Planning Model

The Master Planning Model

The Compression Planning System can be visualized using a master planning model. This model guides you in designing and leading compression sessions. Your timeline, which runs from your design phase through debriefing, indicates how much time you need for your total session.

 Design Phase
The design phase is covered in two steps: design and orientation.

The design of your session is done by the facilitator, and by consulting with your client before your group meets. If the facilitator is your client, he may call on one or more of the group to help with your design, or he may do it himself. This eight-step design procedure is described in Chapter 10.

Orientation, the second step in setup, occurs when you meet with your planning group. Review your design, which is displayed on a storyboard. Be sure everyone is clear on your topic, background, overall project purpose, session purpose, non-purpose, permission meter, and headers. Brief everybody on your background information and artifacts. Explain pureform thinking and review the ground rules for storyboarding.

Breaks are not designed into your schedule except for meals, day's end, and between your exploration and focus phases. Additional breaks are taken when the facilitator or others in your group feel the need. Food and beverages should be easily available.

Let's walk through the eight steps in your planning model:

 1. The Eye of the Needle
This is the checkpoint for the facilitator to assure himself the design is sound and the group is ready to begin working. Your session has passed through the eye of the needle when participants have digested your background, understand your issue, and are agreed on your purposes. When everybody agrees, the needle is properly "threaded," and you are ready to begin generating ideas in the exploration phase.

 2. Exploration Phase
During exploration, your group suspends judgment to explore, uncover, discover, and generate ideas to address your issue. These ideas will later be analyzed, evaluated, and organized into your action plan.

 Break
Take a break to separate your exploration phase from your focus phase. Your break may be short or long, depending on your project, but it must be an unmistakable signal that thinking has shifted from creative to analytical, from exploration to focus.

 3. Focus Phase
During your focus phase, your group analyzes, merges, and selects ideas addressing your issue. The exploration and focus phases may be repeated to generate

more ideas or address new problems. Explore, focus. Explore, focus.

4. Concept

In your concept phase, your task is to pull together your group's thinking and identify the common threads and themes of ideas selected in your focus phase. If your purpose of the session is to deliver five ideas for reducing product returns in half in six months, this is the time to nail down and commit to those five ideas.

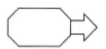

5. Organization

Your group now develops an action plan to put its concepts in play. Your concept and organization phases are your payoff in the process. They describe what will be done, who will do it, and when each task will be completed and expected results.

6. Communications

Your group constructs a communications plan to report on the compression session and the actions that will follow. Communications may be simple or complex, depending on your project. Either way, they should be examined and planned. Your communications board answers the questions: Who needs to know what we are planning? What do they need to know? When do they need to know? How will they be told?

7. Debriefing Board

Before adjourning, debrief on the process and how your group worked together. What went well? What will you do differently next time? What did you learn? Focus on the process, not your content.

8. The Timeline

The timeline along the bottom of the master planning model may cover one hour or less, or it may cover two or three days, even a month or more, depending on your issue. As you work through your design of your session, allocate a target amount of time for each phase of the planning process.

A Two-Hour Session

Design, which is done before your group meets, sometimes takes longer than your session itself.

- Orientation should be brief. Allow 10 to 15 minutes.
- Exploration can be done in 40 minutes.
- Hold the break to 5 minutes, 10 at the most.
- Focus for 25 minutes to get down to the concept for your action plan.
- Organization 15 minutes.
- Communications planning 10 minutes.
- Debrief 5 to 10 minutes.

A Two-Day Session

Designing a two-day session could stretch over days or even months, depending on the complexity of your topic. Your group is through the "eye of the needle" when it knows what it's there to do and understands its method for working together. Plan 15 to 30 minutes for orientation on your project, allow 10 to 15 minutes to explain Compression Planning, and you're ready to go. An exploration phase starting at 8 a.m. usually wraps up by 3 p.m. and then you may start focusing. A focus phase following an overnight break, as a rule of thumb, will run its course by 1 p.m. Within the two days, you may do several small exploration and focus segments. Organization takes about one hour. Communications planning about one hour. Debriefing 15 minutes.

Adjust to Meet Project Requirements

The previous examples are intended as general guides for planning times. Every session will have its unique rhythm and timing. Plan each phase and adjust your time to fit your style of facilitating, the makeup of your group, and your issue.

A project covering a month or six months doesn't require continuous involvement by your group. A series of sessions is used. Between them, the engineer goes off and does her thing. The architect goes off and does his thing. Other team members may consult experts or run benchmark studies. Models are constructed, tests are run. Then your team gets back together, plans, and moves to the next step. Projects of this length rely on diverse planning tools, many of which can be combined with Compression Planning. A number of organizations have told us that without the compression frame of mind, they would never have pulled off lengthy, complex projects.

Chapter 10: Seven Steps To Effective Designs

Of all the basics in the Compression Planning System, your most important is designing — thinking through and planning your session before your group convenes. A great facilitator with a poor design will get so-so results. An average facilitator with a great design can get extraordinary results.

As our Institute has evolved through the years, we have increased emphasis on design. New facilitators who are well grounded in the fundamentals of design learn faster and put the process to work sooner, with better results. So we really work at it.

When the issue is complex, experienced facilitators often test their designs in short sessions with two or three colleagues. The feedback helps maximize your time and potency of your planning group. A refocused purpose statement or a tightened question on a storyboard header card often gives a better flow to the process or unlocks a creative burst from your group.

At the Institute, we teach facilitators to design using our session design form. This is the same form McNellis planning specialists use to design strategic or project planning sessions for clients. Make a copy of the design form on the following page and study it as you work through the seven steps.

You will get much more out of this material if you select an actual project to design as you study these steps. Select one of your own projects. Make it simple. Now is not the time to reorganize the company or develop a strategy for labor contract negotiations. The list of 100 Compression Planning ideas in Chapter 2 will trigger some ideas and help you pick a project. Follow the steps in order and keep reworking them until your design feels right.

Where will you put the design form that's referred to here?

The only way to learn is by designing, so let's begin. Write your client's name on your design form. If you are the client, write your name. Fill in the date of your planning session. Now, step into your design.

STEP ONE: Topic Card

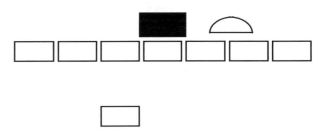

Have you ever been to a meeting where nobody, not even the leader, had a clear idea of what you were there to discuss? Your topic card forces this issue, preferably with no more than 10 words. Stating your topic seems like a simple task. Actually, it can be the most difficult step in the whole process.

Make sure you are clear on the real subject. Be prepared to rewrite your topic card several times. Don't rush.

Your topic statement will be stronger when it begins with a verb ending in "ing" like building - selling – introducing – rolling out - capitalizing.

Nail it down. Use gut-level language. Rewrite your statement any time you realize it is not precise. Make certain everyone in your group is crystal clear on your topic.

Topic cards:

- DRIVING DOWN COSTS OF OUR BUSINESS OVER THE NEXT 12 MONTHS

- STARTING AND RUNNING A MENTOR PROGRAM

- EXPANDING TECHNICIANS' ROLES WITH CUSTOMERS

- GETTING THE NEW LINE UP-TO-SPEED IN 60 DAYS

STEP TWO: Purpose of this Session

Your purpose-of-this-session statements should make clear what your team expects to accomplish during the session. For example, if you want to walk away with three conceptual models for new product packaging, make that your session purpose.

Use one to three subber cards to describe what you are going to work on in this session. Be specific. Begin your subbers with the word "To" and your group will drive for action. When your session ends, participants can say, "We accomplished 'it'" or "we missed 'it'". Working for stated, specific purposes gives energy to your group, drives your whole project, and pulls ideas out of people.

The purposing part of design demands time, effort, and determination, but your return is enormous in focused energy and clear direction. You will find more help and ideas on purposing in Chapter 11. Purpose statements:

- Give direction to your session
- Serve as a point of reference when your group gets off track
- Set the standard against which your group can judge its achievements

Purpose-of-this-session sample statements:
- TO IDENTIFY THE FIVE AREAS MOST NEEDING IMPROVEMENT
- TO FIND TEN IMPROVEMENTS THAT CAN BE MADE WITHIN TWO WEEKS
- TO IDENTIFY SIX AREAS THAT REQUIRE STUDY AND MONEY
- TO IDENTIFY OUR SIX-TO-EIGHT MUST-WIN AREAS IN NEGOTIATIONS
- TO IDENTIFY THE UNION'S FOUR-TO-SIX MUST-WIN AREAS
- TO IDENTIFY FIVE NEW WAYS TO REACH 100 CUSTOMERS IN 60 DAYS
- TO IDENTIFY 10 TO 15 AREAS WHERE THEY MAY BE WILLING TO DONATE MONEY, PROPERTY or OTHER GOODS

STEP THREE: Non-Purpose of This Session

Often your purpose of a session can be clarified by stating your non-purpose of the session and/or project. Your non-purpose is "What we are not trying to accomplish during this project? What do we not want to have happen as a result of our work?"

The biggest one-day Compression Planning strategy session I have ever facilitated was to help a manufacturing organization make a decision affecting 20,000 jobs. The non-purpose of the day was: "To refer the issue back to staff for further study." By stating the non-purpose up front, when the group got to the bite-the-bullet point and were hemorrhaging and looking for a way out, they were forced to make a decision.

The non-purpose drove them back to the purpose of the session, which was to make a decision...today.

Overall Non-Purpose sample statements
- TO POINT THE FINGER OF BLAME AT ANYONE
- TO CONCERN OURSELVES WITH COST AT THIS PHASE
- TO DEVELOP ANYTHING THAT WILL REOPEN THE UNION CONTRACT
- TO DWELL ON THE PAST
- TO INCREASE THE FLOW OF PAPER WORK
- TO CAUSE A STRIKE
- TO OVERLOAD OUR EXPERIENCED EMPLOYEES
- TO HIRE MORE TECHNICIANS
- TO INCREASE THE RISK OF INJURIES

STEP FOUR: Overall Project Purpose

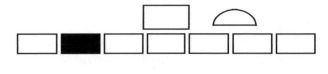

Your overall project purpose should answer questions such as: Why are we working on this project? What do we want to happen as a result of our work together? What do we expect to accomplish?

Purpose statements:
1. TO INCREASE EXCHANGE OF TECHNICAL INFO WITHOUT MORE TRAVEL
2. TO LIMIT PAY INCREASES TO THREE PERCENT WITHOUT A STRIKE
3. TO GET NEW EMPLOYEES UP TO SPEED IN 30 DAYS
4. TO REDUCE CUSTOMER COMPLAINTS FROM AN AVERAGE OF 300 PER MONTH TO LESS THAN 10 PER MONTH
5. TO MAKE CHANGES WITHOUT PRODUCTION DOWNTIME OR OVERTIME

McNellis planning specialists rarely use the words *goals*, *objectives*, *tactics*, or *strategies*. As we go from company to company, division to division, even manager to manager, we encounter different definitions for these words. Therefore, we talk in terms such as "Where are you going?", "What are the 'key moves' you'll make?" "What are the measurements you will use?", or "What steps will you take to get there?" These ideas are later converted into whatever the local terminology may be: goals, objectives, etc.

We apply the concept of "tent-stake planning" in developing purpose statements. The term comes from the technique used in staking down a tent. The idea is to drive one stake as the anchor against which the other stakes are set.

In planning, you drive a specific well-anchored stake (a purpose statement) in your topic and your background. As in tent staking, you may find your first stake is not well grounded, so you pull it up and drive another. In tent-stake planning, even if you don't know the exact spot, you take your best cut and make your overall project purpose as specific as possible.

In designing your session, the facilitator begins by asking the client, "What is your overall project purpose? What do you want to get out of this project?" Your client answers and the exchange goes something like this:

Client: "We want to drive down costs."

Facilitator: "How much in costs?"

Client: "As much as we can."

Facilitator: "Well, how much is as much as we can?"

Client: "We've got to save some real dollars here."

Facilitator: "What are real dollars?" (Keep pushing; don't let up). "Would that be 10 percent?"

Client: "No, we've got to get more than that."

Facilitator: "Eighty?"

Client: "Oh, there's no way 80."

Facilitator: "Fifty?"

Client: "That's way too much on this, but closer to 50 than 10."

Facilitator: "How about thirty or thirty-five?"

Client: "Boy, if we could get a 35 percent cut in costs in this operation over the next 18 months or so, we would really..."

Now you have something specific. The stake is driven. Now, what is your overall project purpose? To cut expenses 35 percent over the next 18 months. Your final step is to convert the 35 percent into actual dollars so we end up with "To cut expenses by $450,000 over the next 18 months."

When your overall project purpose appears vague, such as "to drive down costs," your group can't get energized. That's why we encourage tent-staking. Drive for hard, measurable, verifiable, testable purposes.

In the real world, you may not be able to drive that hard. Some projects just don't produce hard purposes; you can't quite find the specifics in them. More commonly, you end up with a mixture of hard and soft purposes. When you must settle for soft ones, put them on your storyboard and go to work. Often, as you move along, the hard ones will emerge.

If you are not insistent, more often than not

you'll end up with statements like: "The reason we are doing this is to be more profitable," or "To increase our presence in the marketplace." Avoid this mush trap by aiming for those actions causing you to be more profitable or increase market share.

Go for hard, tough, specific purposes, such as:

- To create a one-day response system for customers
- To isolate and dissolve the six key factors blocking one-day response
- To devise six actions we can take in the next 12 months to move from five-day to one-hour response time

These are clear, precise, and measurable purposes that focus your group on what it has to do.

When Specifics Turn to Mush

If your group can't agree on what it will do, your first purpose of the session can be "To determine a purpose for this session," or even "To determine a purpose for the project." Your team may agree: "We know there is an issue to be resolved, but we don't know how to bite into it."

If your purpose can be stated only in vague terms, make the following statement of purpose, so your group will have realistic, if not specific, expectations: "We are here to clarify the purpose of our work on this project."

Agreeing we are not in agreement is one step toward clarity. The purpose of such a session may be "To come out with four or five moves we can make to understand the problem."

Don't give up on being specific with your purposes. Settling for vagueness can be a cop-out. If you can't be specific, keep driving for clarity. What may be obvious to you is not necessarily obvious to someone else.

On Solving Global Issues

Few groups ever meet with the expressed purpose of figuring out how to solve problems beyond their area of responsibility. I say "expressed purpose" because some groups appear to have tacit agreement on global ambitions. Most of those groups disband in frustration, never to fathom why the world would not bend to their wisdom and will.

Those fortunate globe-menders who eventually focus on down-to-earth statements of purpose often end up making a difference. They may realize, for example, their real purpose is "To identify two steps we can take to better equip our salespeople to reach their contacts." Purposing helps you get honest, specific, and focused results. It helps you fire bullets at specific targets rather than fill the air with buckshots and missiles.

Floundering in a Vacuum

Some groups meet, often for hours and days, with no clear idea of what they are expected to do. In the absence of clarity and direction, individuals act on their own prejudices for their own purposes. And why not? What alternative exists, unless they say, "No thank you, I won't attend your meeting"?

Rarely should you consider designing a session as you go. Think it through ahead of time. Nail down your purposes and a set of pathways to get you there, but let your results come from your group. Do not go in with answers and manipulate the group to confirm what your client has already decided.

Can you imagine assembling world-class musicians and having the orchestra leader walks in and announce, "We're here to play Bach. What Bach would you like to play? What measure would you like to start with?" That sounds absurd, doesn't it? But isn't that what goes on in many meetings?

Triggering Compression and Finding Your Way

I can guarantee you after thousands of hours working with groups in planning sessions, the more effective you the designer/facilitator are in discerning and stating your purpose up front, the more effective your group will be. Focused purposing triggers compression. A group moves faster and more effectively when it starts with firm purposes.

Staying Sharply Focused

In your design form, we suggest you write no more than four overall project purpose statements and two to four session purpose statements. If you come up with 20 purposes, that's too many. Combine similar statements and eliminate purposes that are not critical to your project.

If you have too many purposes, your first session can be devoted to identifying your critical questions in your project. For example, "The purpose of this session is to pick out the 8 or 10 critical questions we must answer for this project." That's clear. You ask questions for one hour. Then you sort these questions down to the 8 or 10 most relevant. These can be assigned to members of your team for research and recom-

mendation, or your whole team can work on them.

STEP FIVE: Background

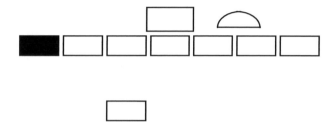

Your background information serves at least six purposes:

1. Background helps define your topic. It includes only the information needed to address this subject. It describes the status quo. Guard against broad generalities that are not fact-based, for example: The field people can't stand the engineering department. Choose instead: The field people hired engineering consultants and bypassed central engineering nine times so far this year.

2. Background orients your group for your sessions and brings latecomers into the action quickly. They can read the basic data while your group continues to work.

3. When the facilitator concentrates on process, background information provides reference points and thinking cues to keep your session focused and moving.

4. Background keeps your data in one place rather than sprinkling it throughout the working storyboards. With background collected, your thinking space becomes an open arena to hear and develop new ideas

and concepts.

Build background for your session by asking your client, "What are the critical bits of information people must know to participate in this session?" Make it thorough but keep it tight. If you have more than one storyboard full of background, you probably have too much background, unless you include artifacts such as sketches, product samples, photos, architectural renderings, etc. Visual references set a tone for your session and help your group understand and focus on your topic.

5. Backgrounding provides the common visual and written information teams need to deal with their issue. All your information doesn't have to be on a storyboard. Products or a piece of equipment can be displayed on a table or on the floor. A photo or model can represent a production center or a new shopping mall.

6. Backgrounding is helpful in toning down the analytical leanings of a group. Some people, particularly if they come out of a high analytical background, such as an engineering department will dig out infinite detail if you don't draw the line. They'll ask, "What color are the fruit flies on top of the garbage truck?"

The color of the fruit flies is interesting and may even be important, but is it necessary? Do we need to answer that to participate in this project? In the early stages, you want people to ask questions to surface relevant information. If new, pertinent background comes up later, it can

be added. Remember, the facilitator's job is to keep your group's energy focused on the purpose of your session.

Start with Agreement on the Facts

Years ago I arrived at a planning commission hearing where two opposing forces were talking about the "northeast quadrant" in which Route 218 crosses Interstate 90 near Austin, Minnesota. Actually, they were at war and the crowd was going crazy.

One group was pressing to buy land and build a shopping center. The opposition was determined to protect a bird sanctuary located in a forest. Both described the property as "the northeast quadrant." After half an hour, I joined the battle: "Mr. Mayor, this isn't my issue, but I'm next on the agenda and I would like to get home tonight. May I say something?" Because we were friends, the mayor said, "Sure, Jerry, what's on your mind?" I walked to a flipchart and drew a sketch of the area in question and labeled the two parcels under discussion. The contest ended. The cannons grew silent. The groups were not even contesting the same ground!

Both areas could be described as the northeast quadrant, but they were talking about different parcels of land. The builders wanted the northeast quadrant a mile or so away where 218 reaches 1-90 from the north. The conservationists wanted to preserve the northeast quadrant where 218 goes south from 1-90. They were fighting a win-win issue – they could have birds and shopping!

This story sounds absurd, but it happened. How many times does something like this go on because the contestants have no common understanding of the facts?

STEP SIX: Permission Meter

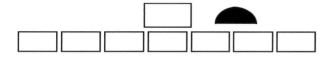

The Permission Meter – cut in a half-round shape to grab attention – normally goes along-side the purpose of your session statements or to the right of your topic card. It's there to re-mind your group of what kind of thinking they have been asked to do. When your meter is set to 1-3 it indicates analytical work, 4-6 suggests discussion and 7-10 is creative. The higher your number, the more creative.

The importance of the "permission level" of a group was brought home to me when I was exposed to research done by the Davies Brickle Group. They studied what goes on in school board meetings and found people are much more effective when cued to what is expected of them on the various agenda items.

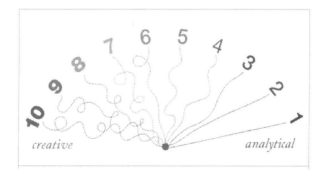

How many times have you sat in a meeting discussing a topic and somebody asked, "What are we supposed to do with this?"

If I tell you, "At the end of this discussion we will make a decision," you listen carefully so you can participate effectively. If you know you're taking in background that will allow you to act later, you listen more carefully and even hold a different posture in your chair.

 The more precisely the facilitator of a session helps participants focus on what is expected, the more effective your group will be.

Make sense?

Change the focus as your group works through a Compression Planning session to sig-nal switches from idea generation, to analysis, to organization, to building a master plan, to designing communications. As the activity ad-vances, change the focus or add a new permis-sion meter on a purpose of your session state-ment where you are working to help your group shift its thinking gears.

Sometimes we use knitting yarn held with pushpins to fence off areas of a storyboard.

In Compression Planning, we are clear and specific in our focus. This eliminates wasted ef-fort and maximizes productive effort.

The idea for the permission meter came from a psychologist friend when I asked, "Why are some groups so creative while others are so mentally constipated that nothing happens?" He explained most adults need permission to act in ways that violate their notion of what is proper and acceptable.

Your permission meter helps groups break through their constraints. When you are looking for unique answers to tough questions, you must have the freedom to probe, listen to your own mind and emotions, and tune into your intuition.

"For many people, this requires permission from outside themselves," my friend explained. So we started using this goofy little device to set free the creativity of Compression Planning groups. The permission meter tells your group what kind of thinking is expected. If the arrow on the permission meter points in the 1-to-3 range, your mode is analytical; 4 to 6 is for discussion; 7 to 10 is "uncork-the-bottle, Harriet, and turn the genie loose." The meter gives your group permission to be creative or to rein in for evaluation and analysis. Here are the general guidelines:

One to Three
A three on the meter calls for loose analysis, your best guess. "This is a $100,000 issue," you might say, or "Between $70,000 and $130,000 is a good guess." Set your pointer at two and you ask for tighter judgment, say "Between $90,000 and $96,000." Setting the pointer at one asks for precision: "Exactly $95,000."

Most Compression Planning groups should not be in the 1-to-2 range. That level of detail should be assigned to somebody for analysis. Don't use group time to crunch stacks of numbers.

Four to Six
The 4-to-6 range is for discussion, those times when you can only sit and talk. This range permits judgment while you are still exploring new ideas, what we call "mixing" (see Chapter

13), but this is mixing with permission.

Seven and Above
A meter set at 7-to-8 allows more creativity: "Whatever you have. Off the top of your head."

In the 8-to-9 range, you start to knock down the premises and assumptions: "If we've always used a five-step distribution system, let's try two steps."

A 10 idea might suggest a one-step distribution system. "We will eliminate distribution in our shop by integrating manufacturing with our distributors' operations. They will buy our technology and handle all distribution." A 10 idea challenges your fundamental premises, the ways you go about doing business. It breaks through the conventional wisdom.

Many people enjoy the freedom of functioning at the 10 level so much they want to use it all the time. This is particularly true when they are inexperienced in Compression Planning. "Isn't this exciting!" they exclaim. Exciting, yes. Productive, no. Reach for 10 on everything and you soon lose stability and continuity. Most issues are resolved in a lower register.

Ask yourself in the design stage, "Do we want to lean into this issue? Are we willing to pull out all the stops and entertain 10-level thinking?" If you are, go for it. Recruit people for your team who are not buried in content and who can rise to 10 when your meter spins in that direction.

Your meter is set with your client's permission and checked with your group. To use the permission meter, your group must be able to tolerate ambiguity because the zones overlap and the focus changes as they move through your session. In practice, the permission meter is helpful in 80 percent of the sessions. At times, I've wanted to throw it out because of the struggle some people have with it. But after they've struggled for a while, I hear, "No, don't throw it out. It may not be exact, but it helps keep us on track in our thinking."

 Our best word of advice on the Permission Meter: When you facilitate, use it for your personal guidance in understanding what's going on in your group. If your group doesn't find it useful, don't force the issue. It can be changed/adjusted throughout your session.

STEP SEVEN: Headers

Develop four to six headers to guide your group through the rest of your planning process and to stimulate their thinking. Phrase your headers as questions where you can. Use active language. Your final header, at the top right of your board, is labeled "Miscellaneous." It is used as a catchall so you don't have to slow down to create a new header when an idea doesn't fit under another header.

TOPIC: How to Doubles Sales of Our Gornblats in the Next Nine Months
- WHAT ARE OUR MUST-WIN POINTS

- HOW CAN TECHNICIANS BE MORE INVOLVED
- HOW WE CAN GRAB THEIR ATTENTION
- WAYS TO PROVIDE SAME-DAY DELIVERY
- WAYS TO GET PEOPLE COMPETING TO HEAR OUR SALES STORY

Everybody struggles with writing headers. It's a skill you can learn with thought and practice — lots of practice. The two basic types of headers are creative/exploration and focus/analytical, with a wide spectrum in between. Creative headers are used during the exploration phase of a Compression Planning session. Analytical headers guide the focus phase.

That is simple enough — creative/analytical. Understanding and using the right type of header is critical to your success as a facilitator. If you're not careful, you can structure your headers in such a way a that leads a group trying to do creative thinking into the analytical thought process. Headers that are too provocative will frustrate a group trying to analyze, sort, and categorize ideas.

CREATIVE / GENERATIVE Headers
Creative headers open up group thinking to new ideas. They remove barriers and get energy flowing. Headers beginning with "Ways to..." or "How to..." ask for creative responses.

Take for example a project whose purpose is "To drive 30 percent of manufacturing costs out of our electric motors annually." Your group might choose to look for $100,000 savings in each part and work toward an overall 30 percent reduction.

These creative headers would work:
- WAYS TO CUT STATOR COSTS
- WAYS TO CUT WINDING COSTS
- WAYS TO CUT BEARING COSTS

Another example: Your project purpose is to penetrate a new market with your products. Specifically, you want to gain a 20 percent share within two years. Creative headers would read:

- WAYS TO GET AN INSTANT GRAB INTO THE MARKET
- HOW TO GET THE BIGGEST PLAYERS LINED UP FAST

Don't automatically convert your purpose statements into headers, even though they give you direction. Characteristics of effective creative headers are that they:

- Cause movement
- Stimulate, provoke
- Aren't yes-or-no oriented
- Are open-ended
- Cause fresh thinking
- Don't have neat borders or limits
- Break down barriers
- Cause excitement
- Get the energy flowing
- Help people participate instantly

In the creative mode, your objective is to get your group moving, so write headers challenging them to reach for answers. To be challenging, ask provocative questions in your headers. For example: "How can we get people beating down our door to do business with us?"

A header stated as "Ways to publicize our project" is wide open for ideas to trickle out, and it may not electrify your group or make them dig for unique concepts. Put steam into your headers. For example:

- HOW TO GET JAY LENO TO DO HIS MONOLOGUE ON OUR PRODUCT
- WAYS TO GET ON THE FRONT PAGE OF THE NEW YORK TIMES

When you put those kinds of headers into your session, you accelerate the energy. Your creativity quotient shoots up a level or two. When you design, ask yourself: What level of creativity do we need to pull off this project? Can we assist the group by writing more challenging headers?

WAYS TO SERVE OUR CUSTOMERS is okay as a header.

HOW TO BE INDISPENSABLE TO OUR CUSTOMERS has more energy.

HOW TO BE VENDOR OF CHOICE FOR THE TOP 15 COMPANIES IN OUR INDUSTRY sets an even higher level of expectation.

That's what you want to think through when you want to put fire into your creative session. If a group is stimulated by provocative headers, there is no way they are going to just sit and listen.

Watch carefully when writing creative headers so you do not trigger an analytical flow. The header "Advertising," for example, will get your group listing types of advertising, which is fundamentally analytical. You'll get radio, newspaper, TV, direct mail, doorknob hangers, billboards, and on and on. When somebody says TV, don't just print "TV" on a card and pin it up. Come back with:

- "What can we do on TV?"

- "Well, we can sponsor the news."

- "What can we do in sponsoring the news that would be special?"

- "We could do a 30-second feature on our company and invite people to call in for a free brochure."

Now you have an idea to try, test, and see if you get the results you're after. Most people find it hard to get going with fresh ideas when your headers are toward the analytical end of the spectrum.

HOW TO GET CUSTOMERS TO LEAVE OUR COMPETITORS AND BEG TO DO BUSINESS WITH US

When you don't know where to put an idea, pin it under your Miscellaneous header. Don't fight over where it goes. Many people love to sit at the table and say, "This doesn't fit in that category. It belongs over there." When that happens they are giving clear signals they are being analytical. If you are supposed to be generating ideas, arguing over where to pin the cards is destructive. Point to "Miscellaneous" and say, "We'll put it here for now and organize later."

ANALYTICAL Headers

Logic and organization are essential in this phase of the planning process. Otherwise, team members can't deal with the material. They can't make judgments. Without logic they will strip their mental gears.

"Who..." headers answer questions about who will be affected, who will benefit, who needs to know, etc. Knowing "who" helps other analytical steps and sharpens the focus of the action planning that follows.

"What..." and "Where..." headers are used to sort ideas from the exploration phase into categories. In this focus phase, the idea groupings are developed into concepts that can be assigned for testing or implementation.

One useful approach for sorting is on a timeline basis, as in Phase 1, Phase 2, or Phase 3. Activities, for example, could be planned for March, April, May in Phase I. Phase II could be June, July, August, and Phase III September, October, November.

Sorting helps to clean up your board and organize the ideas. An idea fits here. It doesn't fit there. Categories may overlap. Don't argue about where an idea fits, just pin it up.

Free-Form Design
When working with a group of high analyticals, unless your headers are quite rich, you can get into a standoff like this:

"That's not a service. That's more of a way to capture the market."

"No, that's not the way to capture the market. That's more a way to improve customer service."

"No, that's a public relations idea."
"No, that's an advertising idea."

Who cares!

All you want is the idea. You don't care what box it fits into. Get the idea, put it in a box later. What do you do when a group starts to play this box-bouncing game? A strategy that works well is to strip away your headers. Capture all ideas, pin them on your storyboard without bothering with categories. Just cook. Let it fly. Organize it later. Put the cards in a circle if you need to, but get the ideas out.

Don't act by rote in designing headers. Stay flexible, tailor headers to fit your design. Let the content drive your headers; don't be wedded to a single approach for everything.

Start with a Design, End with a Plan

A prime responsibility of the designer/facilitator is to center group energy on the purpose of your session and to keep it focused. Although design is important, it should never be so rigid that it becomes a hindrance. Experienced facilitators quickly redesign specific steps when the need becomes apparent.

We have watched many facilitators increase their effectiveness as they improved their design skills. Meticulous design gives the facilitator confidence to go before a group grappling with meaty issues.

Far too many meetings are called by people who say something like, "Let's call a meeting and talk about our marketing plan," or, "Let's get to-gether and think about how to drive down costs in our business." That's like an orchestra leader saying, "Let's get together and try to play some Bach," or maybe, "Let's do some Mozarting" or "Why don't we do some Alicia Keys stuff?"

Design your session and set your storyboards so your team can grasp the problem, understand the purpose of your session, and go to work. You'll be amazed at the difference it makes.

Preparation for Designing and Leading Sessions.

The following list of questions is for interviewing clients. Use it as a guide. You won't use all of them; however, feel free to select those that are useful.

General Background
- Who can you point to who knows the problems?
- Who will benefit or be affected by the outcome of the project?
- Why is this a problem?
- Who are you, and what do you do?
- Tell me about the people who will be at the first meeting. Tell me about the major players.
- Who are some of the key resource people I can contact?
- Who are the key people who can help you with the solution of this problem?

Ecology of the Problem
- At what point did you recognize your organization had a problem?
- Can you give me some background information to help me understand your goals?

- How did this topic evolve to where it is today?
- How long has this been a problem/issue?
- What events led up to this?
- What event or occurrence caused this problem/opportunity/issue?
- What information do the participants need to know before the session?
- What is the most important reason this has become a problem?
- What made you seek help now?
- What are 10 to 12 key points we need to know in order to help you?
- What is the critical information related to this issue? Why is it important?
- What can you tell us about the back ground behind the issue? Tell us what your issue is.
- What things make this a concern to you?
- What important factors do we need to know to help you?

Obstacles
- What obstacles could prevent the project's completion?
- What is your chief worry or concern about reaching your goal?
- Have you ever looked elsewhere to see how a similar or maybe even different type of business deals with this kind of problem?
- What has been done before?
- What ideas do you have that might apply?
- What have you tried or already thought of?

Client Authority and Decision-Making Style
- Who will make all the final decisions in putting this session together?
- Who has the authority or power to do anything?
- How are you authorized to act?
- Would your subordinates see decision-making the same way you do?

Consultant-Client Relationships
- Can you live with the findings or outcomes?
- What outcomes would not be acceptable to you?
- Do I need to submit ideas to you in advance?
- What can I do that helps?
- Why did you decide to come to us?
- What else do you think we need to know to help you?
- What is our "level of authority" to solve/discuss?

Resource Constraints
- Can you sketch out a time table?
- Do you have any deadlines that I need to be aware of?
- How much time do you have to resolve this problem?
- Is there funding to support this project?
- On a scale of 1 to 10, how much energy will you put into it?
- What are the limitations of your resources (time, money, personnel)?
- How much money is available for this project?
- When do you want this problem to be solved?
- What constraints are there?
- What type of a deadline do you have?

Project Purpose

- What's the overall purpose of this project?
- What do you hope to accomplish?
- What can we do to help you accomplish this?
- What topics/subjects do you want to get into here?
- How can we help you now?
- What is your role?
- Describe the ideal outcome of this issue.
- If things were better, what would they be like?
- About your situation, if you could describe how everything should be, what would you say?
- What do you want to do: plan? organize? generate ideas?
- What is your biggest worry concerning this issue?
- What issues would you like resolved?
- What would you like to have at the end of our work together?

Purpose of This Session

- How will we know when we have achieved what you want?
- In our first session with the group, what are some clear-cut, measurable statements that will explain the purpose of our session?
- Please help me understand your goal by finishing this sentence:
  - How can we ... ?
  - What three to five things would you like accomplished as a result of this session?
  - What do you want to be able to walk away with from this session?
  - What do want to leave this session with?
- What do you want us to do for you today?
- What's the purpose of bringing us all together?
- How many solutions would you like us to offer?
- What kind of information do you need?

Non-Purpose of This Session

- What do you not want to happen in our sessions? What areas should we not cover? How might this group get sidetracked? What do you not want us to do today? What issues do you not want to address?
- What do you not want us to discuss?

Chapter 11: How To Focus On Your Real Issue

Purposing is used to focus your group's energy on what they want to accomplish together. Have you ever walked into a meeting and wondered what you were there to do? Have you walked out and wondered if anybody was going to do anything about the problem, whatever it was?

Purposing for Compression Planning is done in three steps: Overall Project Purpose, Session Purpose, and Non-Purpose. Your topic card also helps define your purpose. Effective purposing answers questions such as:

- Why work on this project?
- What do you expect from me during this session?
- What is our collective challenge during this time?
- What do we not want to happen?

Your answers should be specific, not mush. Consider a session in which your purpose is "To do a data dump," to get out all pertinent information on your subject. This purpose is specific in task but general in quantity and quality. Let's pin it down:

- "How much of a data dump?" you ask.
- "Let's try to get to the 90 percent level."
- "Ninety percent of what?" you ask.
- "Ninety percent of whatever we can think of."

Is that a hard, firm measurable purpose? No. But it will put more drive and energy into your group than if you had no target at all. Even that much specificity helps energize your team.

Amazing!

I heard a speaker make the point some years back. He called a woman out of the audience and asked her to hold her breath as long as she could. "Here is my watch," he said. "I'll time you." She held her breath and after 45 seconds gasped for air. "Did you hold your breath for as long as you could?" he asked. "Yes," she answered. "Couldn't hold it any longer?" he asked. She said no, and he challenged her with, "I'll give you a $10 bill if you can hold your breath for two minutes."

She tried again, watched the clock, and held her breath for two minutes. Same person. It was a dramatic demonstration. The crowd was cheering. We were all energized and urging her on. "You won't pass out. Don't worry. Try again." The last time the woman tried, she held her breath for two minutes and 30 seconds!

 That's what good purposing does! It gives you a target. In a Compression Planning session, purposing helps you make the most of your productive time. You get maximum production and creativity in a focused session.

Drive for Fresh Concepts

If you drive for fresh concepts, you tend to get them. If you say, "Let's get together and talk about marketing next year," you may not come up with many creative ideas. But if you say, "We need to come up with two bold moves that will cause our phone to ring 50 times a week from people we've never heard from," you will get an energized response.

Specificity cranks up the creativity. Specific purposes come from a good design by the facilitator or the leader before your session begins. If you sit down with a group and ask, "What do you think we ought to do?" you don't get specific, focused purposes.

Some years back we worked with the young president of a hospital. He was bright and very stressed. Convening his management team in a planning session, he confronted them with this purpose statement:

"To explore optional approaches for confronting the realities of management expenses."

Nothing happened. The group talked a lot but, like the hospital, they were just floundering. I took the boss aside and said, "Tell them in plain language what you saying. Why are we doing this?"

He answered, "I must cut management expenses 30 percent over the next 12 months." He changed the session purpose to read: "To cut management expenses 30 percent." People in the group looked around at each other, and somebody asked, "You want us to do that?"

"Yes. That's what we're here to do."

"Why should we do that?" somebody asked. And she pinned up a card that read, "Why 30 percent?"

He answered, "I can't tell you if it is 26 percent or 35 percent, but I can tell you it's not 6 percent. It's not 50 percent. We must take a big bite out of expenses to protect this hospital." He concluded, "So let's aim at 30 percent. If it's less, good. If it's more, we'll find ways to get more."

The group members understood and were then able to participate even though each one had a big personal stake in the outcome. As they continued to list the "whys," the last statement was, "To avoid the annual Christmas layoff that demoralizes the entire hospital."

Is that a measurable purpose, "To avoid the annual Christmas layoff"? I think so. It's verifiable. That's something to wrap your arms around. Together with the 30 percent target, it helped bring the group to reality. They began to operate within Mike Vance's definition of reality:

"Honesty is the articulation of truth. Truth is the discovery of reality."

This group of hospital managers, when they discovered reality, were focused, creative, and effective. Some groups adjust the purpose statements. They say, "We'll aim at 30 percent and figure out how to get 40."

But make sure your purpose is specific. It's incredible how this will focus and energize a group. You can write down the dollars represented by 30 percent, but how much is "as much as we can"? How many are a few? How much is some? All of these references are meaningless. They don't energize and move people.

Go for Specifics

I'll never forget Kent Colby, who managed a small local radio station in Michigan when I was just getting started as a professional facilitator. Actually, I was moonlighting from my Chamber of Commerce job. Kent asked me to help on a project.

"I'm trying to figure out how to increase sales in July," he explained.

"How much?" I asked.

"As much as we can." He answered.

"How much is that?" I asked. It was a small radio station, but Kent's needs were big.

"I want a $30,000 July."

"How much did you do last July?" I asked.

"$7,200." he replied.

"And you want to do $30,000 this July?"

"Yes!" he said.

So I said to the team he put together to work on the project: "Let's figure out how to do $30,000 in July." You can imagine what it was like with a bunch of radio folks turned loose on a challenge like that. Off the wall! Wild!

Well, they didn't make $30,000. They hit $29,700. Close enough.

That's what purposing will do because you can lean your creativity into it. You can reach for something specific. Some people come from 'the school of thought': "Let's go be creative." The problem is, we don't live a creative life all the time. You're not creatively sitting on a chair reading this book. You didn't creatively brush your teeth this morning because it wasn't needed. Much of our day can go on automatic pilot and that's fine.

We do need to have a creative capacity that can be used when called on. When you want to get the best out of people who may not have had a creative thought in 20 years, have something specific and measurable they can go after. It will help them leap the logic pattern and bridge the killer phrases. If encouraged (and protected) they will begin to challenge assumptions and break down premises. Almost any group will risk their fragile selves for purposes that have stretch and pull.

Chapter 12: Format Designs For Most Projects

The following formations (groups of headers) were developed for addressing some of your most common issues. Somewhere among them is an array to fit almost any situation. You may use them just as they are, but most often you will combine headers from two or more to fit your situation and add in headers of your own. When designing a session, start by leafing through the whole batch. If nothing here fits your issue, design a new formation.

FORMATION 1
Mission for Our Organization

Missioning is key to all other planning for an organization. Because it is fundamental to effective leadership, your mission statement should be constructed by key leaders of your organization.

Once your statement is hammered out, it is a document to be referred to continually. I carry The McNellis Company's statement in my laptop and several times each week I read it and use the statement as my reference point for making decisions.

My experience is groups who are mission-driven tend not to get tied up in morale issues. They pay attention to morale, but they work toward something else. Decision making is easier if you know your mission and your core values shaping it. In many cases, when your mission statement is clear, decisions become obvious. You go back to what you decided when it was written. You're not dealing with your opinion versus someone else's opinion on your present issue.

The headers in this formation all answer the question "What will we be in the future?"

They do not answer the question "How will we get there?"

You contaminate a mission session if you do any "HOWing" on it. Get a clear picture on what, then later put your creativity into planning how you will get there.

> **THE REASON WE EXIST**

This is the time for key leaders to dig deep into their basic, collective understanding of your organization. The emerging statement should be broad enough to permit individual initiative and creativity, yet narrow enough to focus and unify your organization. You may debate over operational details, but don't debate over the fundamentals. Debate over how you are going to do something. The fights should be over how you become an unparalleled organization, not whether your organization should strive to be exceptional.

People all over are trying to draw a bead on what their future is so they can make decisions to get them there. The key to a high-performing system is having a mission driving your organization, a mission everybody understands and supports.

My caution is to refine your statements to a level of specificity. If someone says, "The reason we exist is to make money," that's the obvious first cut, but it isn't your answer because it is too superficial. To make money may be a reason, but it is like saying the reason we live is so we can breathe. See if you can get a more distinct cut: "To contribute 20 percent of our earnings to the parent corporation to springboard our expansion 20 years into the future." That's a more meaningful answer than "To make money."

| THE BUSINESS WE ARE REALLY IN |

This is the question Peter Drucker asks: "What's the business of your business?" The way to look at this is "from a helicopter," where you look down, observe, and X-ray an organization. On the surface, a company appears to be making cookies or selling insurance, but what is the real business of the business?

In The McNellis Company, we look for special conference centers to hold our Institutes and planning sessions. We search for places where the management and staff are not in the business of selling lodging and food. We go to places where their business is to provide and support an environment in which organizational people can learn and make critical decisions. When you understand that's the business you're in versus selling beds, booze, and food, your approach is different. Your scheduling is different. Check-in and check-out times are different. The time you clean hallways is different. Everything is different, from having an understanding of the business you're really in to the essence of what you're really all about.

| OUR CORE VALUES AND KEY BELIEFS |

What are those few core principles you believe in so deeply they drive your actions and take you forward? Look at values you're going to preserve and new ones you're going to take on or adapt. The question to keep pushing: Is each value superficial or does it drive our decision making? Eliminate the superficial.

Focus on your drivers.

| WHAT WE ASPIRE TO BE |

Get this as specific as you can. It is specific to say, "We are a $200-million company and we want to become a $500-million company," or "We are at 30 percent of the market; our aspiration is to become 40 percent of the market in five years." Get your aspirations as tight as you can. Then let your ideas flow from those.

| WHO WILL WE SERVE |

Who are we in business to serve? If somebody says, "The automotive marketplace," that's too broad. Go for specific targets. Are we here to serve new car dealers and fleet operators? Or do we want to serve new car buyers through dealers and fleet operators? There's a difference. To get clear answers on questions such as these is to get better missioning.

| HOW WE WILL BE BEST AND UNIQUE IN 5 YEARS |

I love this one! We will explore our reasons for existing. We will explore how we will be best and unique. The answer today could be different from what it was five years ago, but it still should be grounded in the fundamentals of your organization.

| THE ONE THING WE MUST NEVER TAKE OUR EYES OFF OF |

What is that one thing we must never drop from our foreground? Every business is going to have something different. If you say "customer service," that's too vague.

Massage it. Put some bite into it. For example: "Prompt response to service calls and repairs that solve the problem to the customer's satisfaction the same day."

WHAT OUR TERRITORY WILL BE

This is a geographical question. At a convenience store company I worked with, some people thought their territory should be national. Others thought it should be regional. Some thought it should be east of the Mississippi River. The man who owned the company thought it was a nine-county metropolitan area. They were working off different premises. This can happen which is why you need to get alignment on the fundamentals of the business.

When you get reference points and agreements on what your territory will be, this drives your advertising and distribution, and answers questions such as which freight companies to employ. It tells you what kind of employees to hire. If you're going to do business in the Pacific Rim and you don't have somebody on staff with that cultural background, you may not make it.

This header encourages you to wrestle with where you are going with your business.

HOW WE VIEW OUR MEMBERS

...or Customers, Owners, Stakeholders, etc.) Members is a term many people use to mean "employees." It could be members of your business, church, union, whatever. Your question is, "How do we see them?"

Our staff met over lunch with the person who serves us from the travel agency. We relate to our vendors as extensions of our staff. You function differently when you work through the various groups impacting your business. Be sure to focus on your key groups. Don't list everyone. Pick out the most significant half dozen.

HOW TO WRITE A MISSION STATEMENT

The way to work through the Mission For Our Organization is:

- Storyboard the possibilities.
- Focus by selecting the key statements.
- Break into teams and start drafting the key concepts into mission statements.
- Combine the results into a statement everybody can support.

Make your ultimate objective to come out with fewer than 10 words in your mission statement. Then work to cut and pare it down more. Keep asking "so what" as you prune it. Then work through how to use this statement in your planning documents. I heard of a leader who asked each department and major function to draft three words for their mission. Three words and three words only.

Here's a caution: Don't worry what others will think about your statement. Just make sure it will work for your strategic team. If it answers your questions and brings clarity to your mission, then it will serve you in every aspect of your business.

You may share it with others, you may not. Don't feel you're writing it for somebody else. You're writing it for your own planning and governing purposes.

FORMATION 2
General Planning for an Organization

Every businessperson has seen this kind of planning design. You can do it from the idea point of view: What are your ideas of what our strengths are? Our weaknesses? Threats? Opportunities? What are the trends out there? After these are answered, ask, "What does this data say to us?"

What are our strengths?	What are our weaknesses?	What are our threats?
What are our opportunities?	What does this data tell us?	

Our reason for including this formation is to show traditional planning models that can be adapted. You can take any other planning system and use the compression approach. We are not out to reinvent the wheel – only to improve it.

FORMATIONS 3 & 4
General Situations

These formations are comprised of general situation headers you will want to put into your design kit. They're intended to serve as a checklist. You don't need to use all of them. Try them for master planning, ideas, problem solving, and others.

Who is our Market?	Who is our Non-Market?	Special products/ services we offer

What are we selling?	What resources can we tap?	What are alternative approaches?
Potential hang-ups	Good examples to study	Bad examples to study
What are the timing issues?	What are our concerns?	What are our incentives for customers?
What are our incentives for our employees?	How do we make it interesting?	How do we make it indispensable?
Ways to monitor our progress	Non-traditional things we can do	Our niche could be...
Things we can do no one else is doing	Ways to make alternate approaches work	Ways to activate ideas hanging around
What are the legal issues?	What other industries have similar products?	Premises we are working under
Who is our competition?	"Catchy Phrases"	Ways to tap into resources

FORMATION 5
Marketing

Every project has a marketing aspect. It might be marketing in the classical brand-manager sense, or it may be "We are trying to take this idea from engineering and market it to the field services group." Choose from among these headers to address your marketing issues.

FORMATION 6
How to Improve Anything

This is a way to look at anything you want to improve. For example, you may want to improve:

- A production line
- Work flow on the loading dock
- The annual membership drive
- Time lapse between invoicing and payment

Take a look at what you don't want to change. What should you continue to do? Recognize some things work well and you can keep them as is or make them better.

What are some things we want to start doing and some things we want to stop? (Start and stop should not be just the reverse of each other. Rather, *start* should be: What do we want to start doing that we have not done before?) "We want to start including a vendor appreciation note with invoice payments once each year." After you have done the starts, go to the stops.

If your group is allowed to go through your stop items first, people will focus on problems and your session will go sour. Work your headers in this order: continue, start, stop. Complete each one before moving to the next. This is a good generic approach for a lot of circumstances. Use your miscellaneous header to gather ideas that don't fit elsewhere.

FORMATION 7
Statement of the Problem

This is a general formation that fits lots of situations. Get clear on the statement of your problem and your purpose of this session.

List the parts of your problem. Then sort the parts according to causative parts versus effects. Get all of your parts out. Don't debate your problems – merchandising will look at them differently than human resources; administration will differ with distribution – or you'll end up with arguments.

Sort out all parts of the problem and look at them. As you do, potential solutions will begin to emerge. As you begin to state your problem, solutions will come so keep digging to get clear, distinct statements of the parts of your problem.

Take a break, go over the ground rules of your exploration phase, and then lead your group as it generates ideas. On a complex issue, you may lift out key parts of your problem and make those topics for later planning sessions. Next, narrow down to the ideas you want to implement and move those into a plan that will resolve your problems. Your final step is to make assignments and set deadlines.

FORMATION 8
Provocative Headers

These headers serve in many project sessions. Study the style and write headers with punch to stimulate ideas and raise thinking to creative levels.

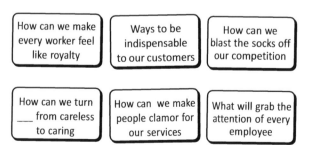

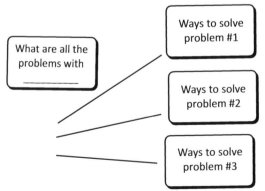

FORMATION 9
How to Improve Receiving Our Raw Materials

This formation, which can be adapted to a variety of situations, focuses on your topic from two directions. From an idea focus, we may go with ideas on how to improve supplier loading. We would like to see items put on double racks, for example, or shrink-wrapped and bound into packages of a certain size.

The other approach, problem finding, is to ask, "What are all of the problems in each of the areas?" You can then use these problems as a springboard for an idea session. "We have identified 100 problems. Let's find the eight or ten most critical ones we can solve now." Make a storyboard from those and dig for ideas under each of the problems.

Your first approach explores creatively for ideas. Your second approach explores analytically to locate your problems. Your headers following "Purpose of This Session" show a linear development of the problem from loading at the vendor's docks to unloading at our docks. Then we add these: People, Timing, and Communications. You may use more headers or fewer.

FORMATION 10
Statement of the Problem II

This is a classic group of headers. Every management process you have ever learned can be married to this formation. If you have learned the cause/effect grid approach, convert it into headers. Formation 10 uses the medical model. What are the symptoms? What are the probable causes? What are the potential remedies? This approach will produce a clean delineation of the parts of an issue from which you can write an action plan.

What are the symptoms?	What are the probable causes?	What are potential remedies?

FORMATION 11
Sorting Ideas After Exploration Phase

This formation is used after you have explored many ideas. Now you are ready to select among those ideas and move into action. Your objective is to focus ideas into a set of workable concepts. Here's the situation: You have one or more storyboards full of ideas. You can work with only six, eight, or maybe 15 ideas, yet you have generated 100 or more. Formation 11 asks: What can we do quickly and easily? What can we do

with some time and development? What must we select for long-term development? These help you sort and make judgments. Set up a separate storyboard or a separate section of a board and use the following headers to sort and choose.

Quick & Easy	Some time, some development	Long-term development (difficult)

Use three headers, don't use four or five. Too many headers gets tedious. When you just don't know enough about some ideas, but don't want to throw them out, create another header: Ideas To Ponder or Items We're Not Sure About or Ideas We Agree To Disagree About.

FORMATION 12
Sorting Ideas After an Idea Explosion

Formation 12 takes another approach to sorting. It asks: What's immediately useful and low cost? What's going to take some time, effort, money? What's a heavy hitter requiring lots of time and resources? You may come up with one or two ideas under every header. These are the ones that go into the concept box on the master planning model. Move these high-potential ideas into your game plan.

Immediately useful & low cost	Some time, effort & money	Heavy Hitter

FORMATION 13
Option Sorting

Use this when you have several discrete options. For example, you can select the Japanese manufacturing system (option A), the American system (option B), or the German system (option C) for your equipment. They all have merit, but you must choose one.

Say you're helping a family select colleges to visit. Out of 50 schools, you've narrowed it down to a manageable three or four. Put up the key points specific to each college so they have visual clarity. Then ask your family to go through and list the strong points of college A. Groups want to go directly to the cons for school A. Don't let them go there! Do all your pros first (A then B then C), then take a break. Come back and then do your cons. When listing the cons, do B first or C, but don't go A, B, C. Some new options may emerge as you visualize your data.

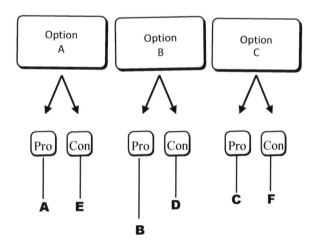

The largest single job I ever facilitated – in number of hours in planning and dollar consequences – used this formation. Another group I worked with faced an issue with eight options. After they had storyboarded through all the pros and cons, one participant said, "This is the first time I have clearly understood the essence of the decision facing us." They had been buried in data. The pro/con approach helped them identify the key considerations to use in making their decision.

After all of the pros/cons were in place, each participant selected the three most critical pros and cons to be considered in making the decision. This helped tone down and focus the data.

While selecting the pro/con choices, we added a header that read, "Tentative conclusions." They wrote their tentative conclusions, talked for awhile, then took scissors and cut off the word "tentative." Their decision was made.

Option sorting can be designed into a session from the beginning, or you may reach a point in your session where you see it's needed. If you so choose, call a break and set up the formation with everybody out of your way.

Some people will look at an idea and say, "That is both a pro and a con." Put it between the two columns or print identical cards for both columns.

In one session with a newspaper client, we had four groups: production, editorial, advertising, and administration. Ideas that came from production were printed on blue cards. Those from editorial were printed on green cards, etc. We could see not only the ideas but also the frame of reference that shaped them.

By using this technique, when you get to a

point where three in your group are for option A, three for B, and three for C, you can go to the A people and ask if they can see any strong points for B. "Can any of you option Cs state strong points for A?" Soon you will find people for option A contributing strong points to B and C, B contributing to A and C, etc. This raises the deliberation to a higher level. Take a quick break. Then go back and do the cons. Most of the time you don't have to go through all of the cons before your consensus becomes evident.

You can move quickly when doing this with storyboards. Your boards give you flexibility; they help groups stick to the point and move to a plan.

FORMATION 14
Coordinating Activities

This design can be used to review all kinds of activities: production and marketing, executive director and board, team leader and members. Always begin with things done well, lest you drop into a complaints and finger-pointing session. Once you review your past and present, move to your future and develop ideas for areas of improvement.

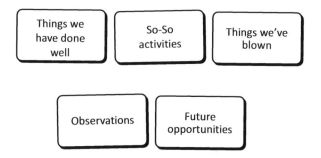

FORMATION 15
As a Result of Our Time Together

These communication planning headers help your group think through your communication needs that flow from its work together. The formation works whether your need is a simple talk-with-my-staff or a communication that requires complex messages and critical thinking.

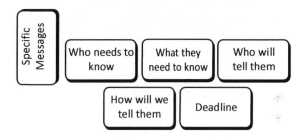

Look to these Formations for Help. When you're first beginning to design sessions, leaf through these formations. You will always get some help. More often, you'll combine parts of several formations and fill in with your own headers. As you get better with practice, you can turn here to jump-start your mind.

71

Chapter 13: How To Dig For Rich Ideas

During the exploration phase, when your group is generating ideas, your facilitator draws out thoughts and helps your group reach beyond the first statement of an idea. He leads them to build on, enhance, and give energy to ideas. We call this "spinning or churning."

The churning process, operating on a scale of 0 to 5, begins with "raw thoughts" at 0 velocity, accelerates them into "rich ideas" at 3 on the scale, and finally peaks at 5 with "formed ideas" that can be assigned to someone, prototyped, cost-estimated, and tested. Effective Compression Planning groups target to spin for "rich ideas" at about 3.5 to 5 on the scale.

I first visualized idea spinning on a Friday night in the Pittsburgh International Airport. While waiting for my baggage, I began to flip coins into a spin pot, a device set up to collect money for a charity. A coin starting down the curved ramp of the pot would spin around the funnel-shaped top until it passed through a hole in the bottom and dropped into the collection bucket below.

It struck me that this is how effective groups develop concepts. They don't just throw out an idea, write it down, and pin it up on the storyboard. They spin the idea until it is useful and there's energy to push it along.

Spin pots can be found in many airports and shopping malls. Watch the coins as they spin. They move down the funnel, gaining momentum until they plunk through into the collection container. By rocking and rotating the spin pot, you can keep the coin going and gaining more and more momentum. For me, the spinning coins represent ideas spinning in a compression group

until they are valid and useful. The analogy is not perfect, but it works.

If you start a second coin down the ramp while the first is still spinning, chances are the two coins will crash and both will drop out of sight. The same is true for ideas. I toss out my idea and before we've dealt with it, you launch another idea. They crash and both are lost. In spinning ideas, we want to launch one thought and spin it to usefulness before starting another. Spin cycles may last only seconds or minutes, but each needs its time.

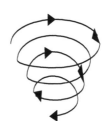 **Spinning in Action**

We teach idea spinning/churning in our Compression Planning Institutes. One small group used spinning to help the vice-president of sales plan a customer relations event. He explained that every year during their industry's biggest trade show, his company sponsored a boat cruise around Manhattan Island for its key customers. Participation had dwindled in recent years, as the heavy hitters declined invitations or sent underlings in their place.

The seminar group was asked to come up with a plan for packing the boat to its gunwales with the right people. The purpose of the session, stated by the client, was to get everyone who received an invitation to accept, travel to New York, and take the cruise.

The first idea out of the group, "We need an interesting invitation," hit with zero impact. The options for the facilitator were to have someone print "Interesting invitation" on a card and pin it to the storyboard or help the group spin the idea into something specific and useful. The choice was made when somebody from the group added: "With a gold seal. It needs a gold seal to give it class."

So the facilitator said: "Let's spin that. What could we do with the gold seal?" Someone said, "Use it to attach the string on a helium-filled balloon." Someone else added, "Put the balloon and the invitation in a box so when the box is opened, the balloon and invitation float out."

"That will get them to read the invitation..." said the facilitator, "So, how do we get them to come to the party?" Someone said, "Let's give a prize. Have a drawing on the boat. Your entry must be brought to the ship in person for the drawing."

Spin: "If you're there and your name is drawn, you win."

Spin: "Win what?"

Spin: "These are big shots we're after. What kind of prize would get them there?"

Spin: "What would make the prize so special they'd be swimming the Hudson River to go on the cruise?"

Spin: "A week's trip to Paris for two. Expenses paid."

Send a gold seal invitation, attached to a balloon, delivered in a giant box, win a week in Paris, expenses paid. Bingo!

All of that came from enhancing the idea that said, "We need an interesting invitation." The group spun and enhanced the idea until they could say, "Got it!" They went from 0 to 5 in about two minutes.

Churning not only produced a rich idea, it also built team energy to make it happen. The idea was workable, could be assigned to somebody to check out, and could be modeled. Costs could be determined. Somebody could assemble a box with a gold-seal invitation and a balloon inside, check out the trip to Paris, and work out a cost estimate. Then management could decide: Is it worth this much to get our top 50 customers and their spouses to our party at the convention? The client was so excited with the plan, he called his office at the first break and got somebody started on the project.

This entire planning session took 90 minutes. Management bought the idea. The invitations went out, and every key customer who received one was on the boat with his or her "significant other."

Ideas in the Group Domain

Spinning cuts through the not-invented-here syndrome. When I spin off your idea, you spin off of mine, and somebody else helps keep the spin alive. We are no longer dealing with "your idea" or "my idea." Every idea becomes "our idea" and has the team's energy behind it.

In a spinning/churning session, don't print every raw idea along the spin path. Spin for rich ideas and clear concepts that can be evaluated and acted upon. Record the end of the spin. Cards with at least 10 words on them clearly indicate good spinning/churning.

This process has to be learned and practiced.

You will find a few ideas will not spin. But your objective is to spin an idea until you can do something with it. An idea is useful when it can be:

- Assigned to someone for action
- Developed into a model or prototype
- Evaluated for preliminary cost and budget

A "workable" idea, like a football, can be passed from you to me. In Compression Planning, workable ideas are usable even though they may not survive in competition with other workable ideas.

Spinning/Churning for Clarity

The supervisor of a manufacturing center described the background for the topic and then began to talk about the purpose of the project. Listen to how the spin works to achieve greater clarity:

Supervisor: "We have a problem with the carts that move products in our plant."

Facilitator spin: "What's the problem with the carts?"

Supervisor: "The wheels."

Facilitator spin: "What's the problem with the wheels?"

Supervisor: "They're not big enough."

Facilitator spin: "Big enough for what?"

Supervisor: "Big enough to roll over the cables on the floor. They get trapped by the cables."

Once the topic was spun to that level of clarity, the solution could be pursued through several avenues:

- Order wheels that will roll over cables
- Remove the cables from the floor
- A combination of the two

There is danger here of losing the intent of the original purpose statement. Remember the client said, "We have a problem with the carts that move products in our plant." Spinning led us to deal with the problems related to the wheels and cables, but does that address the issue? Ask the client.

Facilitator spin: "Are there any other problems with the carts?"

Supervisor: "The spaces between the shelves are all the same but containers are different sizes."

Facilitator spin: "Any other problems?"

Supervisor: "Yeah, the markings on the containers get smudged and you can't tell what they are."

So what's the problem? There are several:

- Wheels that won't roll over cables
- Cables in the way on the floor
- Containers of various sizes
- Aisles that are too narrow
- Poorly marked containers
- Abrasion to the containers and the shelves

The lesson here is: Don't accept the first statement of a problem. Which one does your client want to address? Spin until you are satisfied that all purposes are unearthed.

The Western Mind-Set

The greatest impediment to spinning ideas is that the Western mentality is confrontational, like the boxer who absorbs each blow and punches back. The Eastern mind-set is more attuned to spinning. In the martial arts of the Orient, a participant captures energy from his opponent and rolls with it. Spinning is like that. The group listens to an idea and builds from there, instead of confronting the idea and destroying it with early judgments.

Effective facilitators learn to see the confrontation coming, capture the idea, and spin with the principle behind it.

The "Listing" Mentality

Some of our clients from a giant well-known corporation were taught traditional brainstorming and resisted any suggestion that ideas could be developed as they were introduced. A brainstorming facilitator would ask, "What are your problems?" and participants would list all of the problems, for example:

- "Bearings"
- "Gauges"
- "Fittings

And on and on until the problem well was dry. When the list was complete, they would go back and review each area and ask:

- "What are the problems with the bearings?"
- "What are the problems with the gauges?"
- "What are the problems with the pipe fittings?"
- "What do you mean by that?"
- "What does this say to you?"

The laborious process of going back through all the data buried their energy. They were exhausted before the real issues surfaced. They insisted all of the problems had to be surfaced and then worked through. We persuaded them to try spinning. In a controlled demonstration, half the group gathered in one room for traditional brainstorming. The other half tried spinning workable ideas as they surfaced.

When the sessions ended, a participant from the spinning group said, "With this approach, we could do in three hours what we now do in three days. Imagine what we could do in three days!"

Spinning enhances ideas and drives them to clear concepts. It moves past individual ownership of ideas that must be defended to collective ownership that can be evaluated. This saves phenomenal amounts of time.

"Useful," as we apply the term, is neither evaluative nor restrictive. Useful ideas are those you can work with and do something about. We may agree to develop six or eight workable options and choose one, or we may shoot for 50 useful ideas and select six that have the greatest potential.

When you hear an idea introduced in a group, ask yourself, "Is that actionable? Could I do something with it knowing only what I know now?" If your answer is no or I'm not sure, spin it. Often putting a verb in your idea is all that's needed to make it useful in the sense that you can act on the idea.

The tendency of groups is to *talk* about an issue.

The thrust in Compression Planning is to *do* something about an issue. Spinning helps your group move to action faster.

The facilitator starts the spin and keeps it going by articulating the underlying principle. In the gold-seal invitation example mentioned earlier, the underlying principle was "How can we make an invitation so unique, so compelling, it cannot be refused?"

An Obstetrical Model

The facilitator's role is to help a group deliver usable ideas, somewhat like a doctor helps a mother deliver her baby. The doctor's role is to bring the baby to the place where you can see it wiggle, flop, and cry, where you can count the number of ears, toes, and fingers. The facilitator's job is to help your group spin an idea to the point at which it can be understood, accepted or rejected, acted on or set aside. In the process, there are times to be gentle and times to be aggressive and firm, but your objective always is to deliver the idea.

The obstetrical model is a good one to keep in mind. The doctor or the midwife doesn't have to like or dislike the baby. That's not his or her responsibility. The job is to get the baby delivered.

In meetings, we often go into the idea mode as if we're going to deliver a 17-year-old child who can drive a car while simultaneously doing his math homework and talking to his girlfriend on his cell phone. Your real task is to conceive the idea, move it along, and get it delivered to the point where it can take on some life, breath, and energy. That's the model effective facilitators follow. Spinning helps deliver the baby.

In a creative session, your objective is to get one idea safely delivered and then deliver another, and another, and another. Some will pop out fully formed in seconds. Some take two or three minutes of labor. But when each "delivery" is finished, you will have a usable idea.

Chapter 14: Try The Squid, You May Like It

Unique is a word that is seldom used in its strict definition: one of a kind. Today, unique means unusual, a standout. The mind is attracted to "one of a kind" as a concept. At the same time, it is repelled by one of a kind if this "unique" is outside our pattern of logic, our experience, our conditioned way of viewing and looking at things.

I was introduced to the concept of uniqueness by my father. I'm not clear how it matured in my mind, but I came to associate energy, excitement, efficiency, and effectiveness with unique.

The superstars in business don't do what others do in the way others do it. Almost by design, they go contrary to others' methods and goals. A lot of what they accomplish is behind the scenes – things you don't see. Their systems are better designed and they execute better. How they hire, recruit, train, fund, acquire, and structure – as well as the on-stage things you see in their marketing – are beyond the ordinary. Only in retrospect does the unique appear obvious.

In a Compression Planning session, the degree to which your group can think in terms of uniqueness is influenced by the extent to which they can relax in their thinking. When a person offers a unique idea, it is often at a stage where no data is available to support the concept. It is new. It's never been done before. The only way to know if it will work is to construct a model and see if it works.

I don't think you should try to reinvent the world on everything. That's why I'm not for "the wilder, the better" approach many people advocate in brainstorming. That may be okay for some problems, but if you're trying to reorganize your loading dock, you're not looking for wild ideas, at least not what most people call wild.

At one time, a forklift was a wild idea. Having a telephone on the loading dock was uncommon. Now hanging a cell phone on a forklift on the loading dock is common practice. A few years ago, it would have been unique.

In a Compression Planning session, without tolerance nothing new will be discovered.

Some people will take the position every idea is usable. That's ridiculous. Every idea is not usable. Lots of ideas are stupid. How do you find out if they're stupid? Put data on them. For example, research may show somebody tried what you suggested 50 times, with the result that 49 out of the 50 times it failed. That's data. All too often people kill ideas by laying on opinion instead of data – what they think, not what they know.

We shouldn't avoid making judgments, but the judgment ought to be: Should we take it to the point of gathering more facts, more information? How often do people sit there and say, "The old-timers won't go for it"? Well, that's an opinion. But if you run it up the flagpole and 100 out of 100 old-timers shoot it down, you can believe and act on that data. What if 30 go for your idea and 70 don't? Maybe you should try it and take the next step.

Putting Energy Behind Ideas

A little-appreciated phenomenon that gives life to rich ideas is the energy put behind them. Think of it this way:

Idea x Energy =
Long-Term Meaningful Results

Quality is a great idea, probably 5 on a scale of 1-to-5, but what makes a quality program work is the energy behind it, not the idea itself. Quality is an idea that succeeds because the CEO emphasizes quality in every message he sends for the next 50 years and backs it up with standards, investment, training, and supervision. When responsibility for quality gets written into the commitment of every employee, it becomes a reality. That's when the formula Idea x Energy = Long-Term Meaningful Results produces big numbers.

In a Compression Planning session, the unique answers are frequently already known. You see them in retrospect. Often people have been talking about them for months or years, but they never got enough energy packed into them for anything to happen.

But someone else will take that "unique" idea, put energy behind it, and be successful. The idea can embrace a product, a system, a program, an entire company. Get the data on 100 dentists and you'll find one or two stand head and shoulders above the others. Out of the 100, some are going to be starving and some will do well.

Let's take a hypothetical class of graduates from the Dental School at the University of Pittsburgh. Observe those who set up private practices and do well. They'll do things the others don't do, things the people in dental school told them were crazy.

It may be something as simple as the dentist who, after he does a root canal, calls you at home that night and asks how you are doing. How do you feel about his call the next day? What do you do? Tell your neighbor.

Now, if all dentists start calling after root canals, this practice becomes standard and loses its uniqueness. Then what does Dr. Standout do? He looks for something else unique or finds a way to do what everybody is doing, just better.

Mustard! Look what happened to mustard. A few years ago, someone repositioned mustard in the market. Instead of selling big jars for less, they sell small jars for more. They throw in a few extra spices, herbs, a dram of wine, and they call it Grey Poupon. They hire an actor to speak with a British accent. Instead of somebody saying, "Please pass the mustard," he says, "Pardon me, do you have any Grey Poupon?" "But of course."

They have created a unique marketing concept. You go to the store and see several brands of yellow mustard. Who's up there with Grey Poupon? At first, no one. They were unique. Now there are copycats. I don't know this for a fact, but I'll bet the cost of Grey Poupon ingredients aren't much more than the others. They just market a smaller package with an English accent and sell it for more. By thinking "unique," they broke out of the price competition.

Successful businesses look for a unique edge because if they don't, what must they do? The only answer is to compete on price. Charge less. When most competitors pursue the low-cost strategy, how do you maintain your price? You don't. You cut it to compete.

I encourage everyone to explore uniqueness. Look for it. Unique is not superficial. If someone says, "We give good service," that is not unique! That's a shallow answer. There's no spin on it. But this guarantee: "We put your breakfast hot on the table in your room within seven minutes of the time you order it," is unique. It has spin energy. Most unique concepts evolve from spinning ideas around focused objectives.

A Mass of Barriers

As you search for uniqueness, a mass of barriers pile up in the way. Among these barriers include tradition and logic, not Aristotelian logic, but the logic you and I set up in our brains of the flow, sequence, and appropriateness for doing things.

We eat salad before dinner in the U.S. In some countries, they eat salad after dinner. Probably somewhere else, salad is eaten after dessert. That violates something in our brain, but it's not the fundamental of our brain it violates. Salad after dessert wouldn't violate a three-year-old's logic. It violates a pattern educated adults have set up I call "small-L" logic." It's not logic in the sense of major premise, minor premise, and conclusion. We say, "That's illogical. It doesn't make sense. That's nonsense." It is "non-sense" in that it is not sensible, and sensible means rational. It is not logical. That's how it appears to us.

I maintain the only answer to whether or not an idea or a product is logical lies in the marketplace, not with you and me sitting at a table thinking. We may create the greatest product on the face of the earth, but if it doesn't work in the marketplace, it doesn't work. The important step is to get it out there and see how the market reacts.

Aim for 60 percent improvement. Don't aim for 100 percent perfection. Test. Later, improve it again by 60 percent. Add up the increments and soon you're up to 96 percent. That may not be 100 percent perfection, but it's not bad, especially when you consider how many people study a new concept to death. Compression Planning isn't based on 100 percent. It says, "Make it better. Make it considerably better if you can, but make it better. Move it!"

Unique in Heavy Traffic

This incident happened in Jacksonville, Florida, when I responded to the knock on my hotel room door.

"Hello, Mr. McNellis. I'm Hank, your cab driver," said the man who stood in the opening. "Let me have your bags. I'll put them in the car and wait while you check out."

I found the driver at the curb, where he opened the door and smiled me into his cab. The car was immaculately clean outside and in. A Dustbuster was under the front seat. Fresh linen on the back of the seat provided a spotless area to rest my head.

Hank asked the usual questions regarding what airline, time of departure, where I was headed, etc. Then he wanted to know, "Do you have a business card, Mr. McNellis?" When I explained I had given out my last one, he asked, "Well then, will you sign my guest book? I'd like to put you on the mailing list for my newsletter."

I signed in and commented it was unusual to have a cab driver call at your room. Unique, you might say.

"That's the way I run my business," Hank offered. He schedules appointments like mine and supplements those by waiting in the queues. "Lots of drivers," he said, "waste a lot of time waiting in lines at hotels and airports." Excited about his services, Hank explained he is an independent driver. He subscribes to a radio dispatch service, or appointments can be made by calling his telephone answering machine at home.

Does he make any unusual appointments, I asked. Well, no, but he does deliver kids to the orthodontist and return them to their schools. On Saturdays, he picks the kids up at "her house" and delivers them to "his house." Sunday evening, he returns them to her house. Here's another angle he described. Let's say we're working at the office and need some special supplies. We could interrupt what we are doing, get them, and pay the price in lost time; or we could call Hank and pay him to run the errand.

At the airport, Hank carried my bags to the check-in counter, inquired to see if the plane was on time, and wished me a good journey. "Let me know the next time you're coming to town and I'll pick you up." He handed me his business card, shook my hand, and walked away with a generous tip.

Unique? Certainly unusual. Here you have a cab driver in Jacksonville named Hank who drives an immaculate cab and wants your business. In this day and age, just finding a clean cab is unique in the broadest sense of the word. How many cabs have you found that were dirty? So what does that do? It creates opportunities for ingenious souls like Hank to serve people who want to ride in clean cabs with drivers who want their business.

Hank looks at the market differently. He has "naive eyes." I'm sure he didn't come to this business concept full bloom. He tried some things to see if they worked. He tried appointments, for example. When they worked for business people going to the airport, he made that part of his operating practice, and he extended the principle to other opportunities.

A lot of unique ideas come from people who look with "naive eyes." They don't know an idea won't work, so they meander in to find out what the data tell them. This is what Carl Sagan calls "post-judicial thinking." This is thinking done after you have explored, made a model, and tested the concept. With data, you can make an informed judgment. Take a simple thing like squid pizza. Like it? Nine people out of 10, probably more, will answer, "Are you kidding? No way!!" They don't refuse based on data. They just know they don't like it. Take a bite and you'll have data.

The key in searching for the unique factor is to suspend judgment until you have enough data to make an informed judgment. Translation: Try the squid – you may like it.

Chapter 15: How To Warm Up A Group And Keep It Hot

One role of the facilitator is to ignite your group's energy and keep it focused on your issue. In short, keep the creative juices flowing. The Compression Planning System, which is designed to keep your team focused and moving, is itself an energizer. Your facilitator also has available a number of techniques and aids for picking up the pace and re-energizing your group.

Many facilitators like to use vigorous mental or physical warm-ups to deliver a jolt, shake 'em up, and get 'em moving. Others use a gentler touch. Both get results. Whatever the style of the facilitator, warm-ups should be chosen and timed to help your group achieve its purpose.

Getting Loose

Some facilitators have the gift to relax, joke a little, rev up the energy, and move along. Others prefer a pragmatic approach, leaving little space for humor. Every facilitator has a style. Most of them work. Yours is right for you. Go with what's comfortable.

Compression Planning gets people involved. It gets them up and moving, physically and mentally. The storyboards help to focus your group's attention and energy on your issue.

Humor is a tremendous aid in relieving tension and energizing people. Over the years, I've noticed after people laugh a couple of times, I relax and so does everyone else. For me, or any facilitator, to start a planning session by telling a joke seldom works. Anyone struggling to be funny usually lays an egg. Some people are naturally funny. They don't tell jokes, they just make you laugh and join the fun.

Humor comes from unexpected sources. If you have a hand in recruiting your project team, look for someone whose natural style helps people stay loose and keep cooking. Such a person can make contributions well beyond his knowledge of your issue. A sense of humor is a godsend when working with groups, but it is not essential. Many effective facilitators don't use humor.

Trust the people in your group. If you set the stage, get the process rolling, and give your participants a chance, they will help move it along. Somebody printing a card misspells a word and your group goes ape, even though you stress spelling doesn't count. I like to give somebody scissors and a card to cut out an arrow or two. Somebody else will cut out a shape that looks like a wart hog. Either way, everybody laughs and the tension melts.

It seems effective groups always reach a stage of struggle where they turn to laughter. And they are then released to deal with difficult issues and express their frustrations, ideas, feelings, and hopes.

Every able facilitator has a bag of tricks and techniques to help the process. Physical activity is great. Something as simple as a stand and stretch can revive the group's energy. I tell people, "Stand up and wiggle." They wiggle and giggle. Then they are ready to get back to work.

One difficult session involved nurses and doctors. We did no warm-ups the whole time because I sensed that doing so would have violated their feelings about the issue and each other. They needed the release, but they wouldn't have accepted it.

High-performing groups demand release of pressure, and they re-energize themselves. One of my favorite clients, the president of his company and a motorcycle enthusiast, inspired this warm-up: "Everybody imagine yourself straddling a bike. Now you're sitting in the saddle. Wrap your hands around the handlebar grips and twist. Varoooom! Varoooom! Do a wheelie." You know it's impossible to do that without smiling and acting a little goofy. You are now ready to roll.

Combining breaks and thinking works, too. Pairing off participants and telling them, "Take a walk and come back in 10 minutes with five ways to..." It stretches the muscles and fresh new ideas will surface.

Here is another approach: "We need to get energized. Just to get our brains going, in two minutes let's come up with 50 ways to improve a hot tub."

Or try this: Take off your shoe and ask, "What can you do to improve this shoe?" Your first answer always will be: "Deodorize it." It doesn't matter whose shoe it is, everybody laughs.

Get a free-for-all going. Get a little rambunctious.

Getting Started

Mental exercises get groups off the ground. Spend two or three minutes throwing out ideas on ways to improve something, such as 50 ways to improve a ballpoint pen. What are all the ways we can think of to improve a pair of glasses? Seventy-five uses for disposable diapers other than their primary use?

At one time we used warm-ups at the beginning of sessions. But 8 out of 10 groups don't need warm-ups on the front end. Often doing so seems contrived. Picture this: You walk into the room and say, "The group's purpose is to improve accounts receivable during the down period when everybody is on vacation. But before we do that, let's get warmed up. Everybody stand and quack like a duck." Sound absurd? It is!

One of the most emotional topics I've ever worked on was when working with the National Sudden Infant Death Syndrome Foundation. You can imagine the intensity of the emotions. One doctor told a joke concerning his mother-in-law. All through the session when emotions would surface and everyone was beginning to be uptight, he would say something such as, "What do you think my mother-in-law would do about this?" and everybody would laugh. Healthy groups create ways to stay energized, to stay loose. The facilitator doesn't have to force it, only help it along.

Reminder Balls

The most effective device we have found for releasing tension, energizing, accelerating, and loosening up groups is a little item we call reminder balls. The idea sounds dumb but it works.

Made of soft foam, our reminder balls are the size of a tennis ball. The name is derived from the "phrases" – those not-so-bon mots people drop when they hear a fresh idea. You know the ones: We've never done it that way before. It's not in the budget. Sometimes "zapper" phrases don't have words. A look over the top of those half glasses that are standard equipment for new vice-presidents says volumes more than mere words.

The use of the balls must be prenegotiated with the group. Everybody has to agree when someone drops a phrase or ignores another ground rule, anyone is free to roll or gently hand a ball his way. The response is laughter and released tension. These little spheroids are effective in shutting off long speeches or deflating pompous egos. The more senior your group, the more effective they are.

Just having reminder balls on your table makes a point. People start to roll them around and bounce them off each other. Their effectiveness is derived in part because they are tactile. They are physical, yet when you bounce them off somebody, they don't hurt.

Some participants use them to play handball during breaks, a mild form of exercise that eases tension. Others will take a yardstick and practice their putting. The balls are like executive toys. They give nervous, fidgety-types something to do with their hands.

Ninety-five out of 100 times, a group functions better with reminder balls, or something serving the same purpose. In the other five percent, your client doesn't want them or they backfire. When this happens, you may discover a lack of trust or another dysfunction in your group. In rare instances, you encounter pathological issues. Listen to your intuition; it will tell you when problems lurk. Don't make a big deal out of using or not using reminder balls.

Thinking Cues
Groups may need mental prompting when their thinking gears grind to a halt. Thinking cues start your ideas flowing and then keep them rolling. Cues come in two varieties: **content** and **process**.

Content cues come from knowledge in relation to your topic. Referring to information displayed under your background header will take you back to content. Reviewing your purpose headers also will also take you back to content, jump-start your group's thinking, and start it moving again. Content cues come from selecting a piece of information and massaging it with questions such as: What else can we do with that? How can we enhance it?

A hyper-energized facilitator will ask a question, then another and another, and never pause long enough to allow an answer. This comes with an adrenaline high, or when the facilitator loses confidence in himself or the group. He will get quite animated and say (not ask): "Now tell me what we can do with that." Your facilitator doesn't get an immediate answer, so the question must be wrong. Better ask another question: "What else can we do? How are you going to do it? What else?"

Even bright people can handle only one question at a time, and even they need time to think. A group functioning spontaneously may not need any questions. That's the time for your facilitator to be quiet and let it flow. Silence can be a powerful thinking cue. Ask some questions. Leave some space.

From Mike Vance, I learned to use the natural senses of sight, sound, taste, touch, and smell as thinking cues. Try it now in the room where you are reading. What ideas come to mind as you sense your room and think about how to make it more functional? What do you hear? What are your touch sensations? How does it smell? What do you see as you examine it in detail? Think through any issue with your five senses and you'll gain new insight.

A •) • B The Arc concept is another thinking cue that will help you switch perspectives and be more creative. The concept is an arc looks concave from one side, convex when viewed from the other. To apply this principle, ask questions from one side of the "arc" and then another: How would our customers approach this subject? Our vendors? What would impress a six-foot-four-inch person who is checking into our hotel? A small child? How can we reach the first-time business traveler? The veteran business traveler?

Validation is another thinking cue for gaining new perspective. If your group is working on an issue involving a production center, go to the work area and five-sense it. Or, ask yourself how you would view it from the position of operator, maintenance person, scheduler? Stand where they stand and think about it. Study it from your customer's perspective. Would you want to buy something made in this production center?

I was once asked to help a hospital staff rethink its obstetrical admissions procedure. We decided to validate the experience by going through the procedure. One member of the team agreed to play the new-mother role while the others observed, asked questions, and took notes. To get a different perspective on the issue, our "new mother" was a man. Think about that. You can be sure our "mother" had a new perspective after he was dressed in a hospital gown and told to put his feet in the stirrups of the examining table.

Other unusual validations we've done: touring a sewage treatment plant, moving an ingot of metal through a rolling mill, riding in an automobile as it sloshes through a car wash.

Symbolizing is another powerful thinking cue. Ask participants to draw, in 20 to 45 seconds, their perception of their organization today. Follow up with their drawings of how they want the organization to function six months from now. Symbols say a lot in a little space and time. Potent symbols communicate instantly.

The thinking cues you employ influence the outcome of planning. As a design exercise in our Compression Planning Institutes, we use a problem of a landlord who wants to increase occupancy of his apartment building. When we first began to use this example, we gave the groups, which assumed the role of the facilitator, a lot of background and time to interview the landlord and fill in the gaps.

We now start the exercise without background except to say this man has an issue he wants you to help him solve. He heard you are bright facilitators with a process that can help him. The assignment is to interview him and design a Compression Planning session. The facilitators have eight minutes to think through their questions.

We get better questions when the exercise is set up without background than when we say, "Here's someone with only 55 percent occupancy in his apartment building and he wants to build it up. What are your questions?"

When teams start with content, they go after more content. How many apartments? How old are the tenants? What's your competition? All this is important information for addressing the issue, but not helpful for designing the sessions. Content-focused facilitators often forget to nail down the answers that will help them design to address the client's needs.

The groups without background information ask general questions to help elicit information. They come out with better focused, richer, more provocative questions, such as: "Tell us the 10 to 12 key facts about your issue we should keep in mind to help you."

"What would you like to have in hand when you leave the planning session?" These are questions that help your client and the facilitator think about the issue in creative directions.

High-Energy Planning time
A lot of groups work at the wrong time and pay the price in the form of low performance and exhaustion. They'll start a session at 4 o'clock in the afternoon when they are brain dead. They would be three times more effective at 8 o'clock in the morning.

Give your issue the absolute best time you have, especially if you're doing strategic thinking. When you make seminal decisions to take your organization three, five or ten years out, give it your best time. And don't hitchhike onto other activities.

Thinking is exhausting work. Compression Planning is doubly exhausting. An enormous amount of psychological energy is consumed when people make crucial decisions. Also, listening is exhausting, and good group planning takes a lot of listening.

Chapter 16: Forging Clear Concepts From Rich Ideas

The task of your group in the Focus Phase is to sort through all ideas on your storyboards and focus them into a few clear concepts your group can act on. Zero in on those workable and useful ideas – your keepers that move your project forward.

The preliminary sorting method used most often in Compression Planning is called "dotting." Dotting is a helpful technique planning teams use to select, isolate, and focus ideas. Your group's task is to identify your unique and high-potential ideas that are pivotal components of your issue. Each person reviews the data and makes choices. During the final convergence of ideas into concepts, everybody is up to speed and ready to participate.

Here's how it works: After your break is taken to mark the shift from the Creative/Exploration Phase to the Analytical/Focus Phase, everyone in your group is given an equal number of self-sticking, colored dots. (We use removable labels, 1/2-inch in diameter.) Everybody is instructed to stick dots on ideas with the highest potential. Each team member dots without consulting others or studying their selections. Everybody may dot the same cards, but each person may place only one dot on a card.

A rule of thumb for the number of dots per person is one dot for every 7 to 10 ideas on your storyboard. One hundred ideas, give each person 13 to 15 dots; 50 ideas, 7 or so dots. If you have only 20 or 30 ideas, don't give only two or three dots; hand each person four or five, but don't use 15 dots on 30 items.

A fine point, but one essential to observe: stay away from voting terminology when you describe the sorting process. If your team gets into voting (four are for this idea, three are against), you may destroy the cohesiveness of the team. One company we work with calls the dots "energy bullets." Their objective is to mark ideas carrying the greatest group energy and commitment.

 If your team is divided into groups with special interests, you can give one group red dots, another blue, and another green. Later, when all of the ideas have been dotted, the influence of special interest can be evaluated. You may have your client dot in one color and the rest of the team in a second color. Your home office people may dot in red and field people in green; engineering in one color, manufacturing in another. However, if this is a low-trust group, don't use a variety of colors. The colors will tend to emphasize the differences.

A concentration of dots shows where the energy is focused, but this is not pure. Some people will follow their leader in making choices. When your boss puts a dot on an idea, they dot with the boss. If you sense your group is not high on trust, ask your boss to dot last. If it is a high-trust group, nobody will care what your boss does. Everyone will do her own thing.

After the dotting, sort the ideas. Start with cards that have the most dots. "This one has seven dots, and there are seven people. Obviously a keeper, one we want to go forward with. Everybody agree?"

Before you begin to sort, print the word "retrieval" in capital letters on a large clasp envelope, bend back the flap, and pin it to the storyboard. Any ideas the group decides are low in potential or don't "fit" should be placed in this envelope. Remember, if you throw an idea away, somebody's ego goes with it. Give the retrieved cards to the client for possible review later.

Some people will want to reorganize the storyboards before they start dotting. Resist this suggestion otherwise you risk ending up in a wrangle and wasting a lot of time. Everyone will see a different set of categories and start to argue over which idea goes where. If an idea explosion has left your boards in disarray or they must be reorganized for some other reason, ask one or two volunteers to reset the boards while the others take a break.

An item should not be tossed aside just because it doesn't get a dot. An undotted item, after more reflection, analysis, and evaluation, may end up being your best idea. The one with the most dots may end up in retrieval. But dotting gives you a place to start sorting.

Before dotting, go back and review your purpose headers. What are we here to do, on this project, in this session? Tell your group to place dots on ideas with the highest potential consistent with your session purpose.

Another Approach to Sorting

Ideas may be sorted under your headers without dotting. If this is your decision, ask your group: "Which header shall we start with?" Someone will answer: "We better pick out our target audience before we go after services." Take your group through the ideas listed under your target audience header. Lead them in making judgments, move high-energy ideas to the top, set aside others. Does this fit? Should it go?

Should it stay? Move fast and get your ideas pared down to a manageable few. Then move on to your next header. After a bit, logic will take over and concepts will emerge. A new header may be needed.

When we were planning the move of The McNellis Company to new office space, a surprise issue arose. We had narrowed the choice of buildings to three or four by sorting according to square footage, lighting, shipping, access, partitions, storage, and other essentials. The question of personal safety never came up. Then one day, a local newspaper reported a break-in and some extreme violence across the street from the high-rise building we were considering.

From that moment, personal safety became a major consideration in our selection process. So we added it as another sorting factor, thus eliminating the high-rise. Then we discovered a building that wasn't on our list. It checked out highest on all the sorts.

Generating More Ideas

During the sorting, you may lift out three or four ideas to become headers for generating more ideas. For example, in a project to develop a new distribution network, these new headers were introduced:

- SYSTEMS CHANGES WE CAN MAKE
- WHAT OUR VENDORS CAN DO FOR US
- CONTRIBUTIONS OUR CUSTOMERS CAN MAKE

The team didn't start out with these headers. They describe patterns that grew out of the ideas under other headers. Move ideas that fit under your new headers, generate more ideas if appropriate, sort the final group, and make your selections.

While developing one concept for addressing an issue, conflicting concepts may come out. If this happens, collect the ideas under the various concepts. Here are concepts in a marketing plan:

- Concept 1: Using a dealer distribution system
- Concept 2: Direct sales to the market
- Concept 3: Using an agent or brokerage system

Sort your ideas under each concept and then evaluate your concepts. If one idea fits under two concepts, make two copies of the card. For more ideas on sorting, see Chapter 12.

In Compression Planning, the team producing lots of ideas must also be tenacious in paring them down. Remember the "elegance principle": "A few simple ideas done well are much more powerful than a ton of things done poorly."

I learned the elegance principle from the executive director of the Rose Bowl. He told a convention workshop, "Here we are, the biggest and the grandest of the bowl events. Yet what we do is rather simple. We focus on just three activities: choose a queen, stage a parade, and play football. After the game we throw a party for everybody who worked on the projects to celebrate and thank them for their commitment."

"With all our people and resources, and national attention, we concentrate on three activities. We put all of our energy into those. You hear about a little festival in Buffalo Creek on the Great Plains and they plan 85 events to celebrate their bicentennial. Later they can't understand why 83 of them ended up buffalo chips."

He explained that the good people of Buffalo Creek don't have the resources to do more, yet they are driven to try because they think that's what "the Big Boys do." Even giant General Electric can't attack on every front. Their problems are the same as the one-horse operator when it comes to elegance. The Big Boys can't do everything well. When they try, they fall short of their goals.

 The most effective teams are disciplined in selecting the elegant ideas with the highest potential and moving with them.

Chapter 17: Putting Your Plan To Work

The objective of Compression Planning is to develop and commit to a plan that will advance or resolve your topic. The purpose of the Organization Phase of the process is to "keep alive the output of Compression Planning." In Chapter 8, we describe "all-at-onceness thinking." The organization board is all-at-onceness tracking. The board keeps in front of your group those tasks they have committed to do.

The formation employed most often to design an action plan has three headers:
- Tasks
- Who will do it/Deadline
- Expected Results

Tasks

When working with these headers, list all of your tasks first. Get these out by asking a question such as: "What are we going to do to pull off this plan?" Don't use general terms such as: PLAN THE CAMPAIGN or COMMUNICATE WITH CUSTOMERS

Instead, be specific in describing what is to be done:
- Draft Letter to Employees
- Get Three Printing Quotations
- Select a Distribution Vendor
- Get Bids on Three Meeting Locations

Don't make a list of what could be done. Focus on those few actions that must be done for your plan to succeed. Ask your group, "Are we going to do all these? What should be eliminated? Should something be added?"

Who Will Do It/Deadline

Once you agree on your tasks, prioritize them. Point to each task and ask, "Who wants to do this?" Many tasks will have a natural home in your group. The director of marketing has to take on certain jobs, your director of engineering others, your systems person another. Some jobs, however, can be handled by anyone. Your key to success in assigning any task is to find someone who is capable and wants to do it.

When somebody agrees to take on an assignment, have him sign a card (not just print the name, but sign it) and pin the card on the board. It then becomes a signed commitment to complete the assignment.

Deadline

Next ask, "When will you have this done?" Go for a specific date. Pin the date on your board next to the task description and the signature of the person responsible. Don't settle for something vague like, "Oh, in about two months."

The deadline and Who Will Do it can both be printed on one card.

Expected Results

You want to look at each of your tasks and ask the question, "what is the specific, measurable, verifiable deliverable we will see as a result of this task?" Each task should have an Expected Result that gives even further guidance to the person tackling the assignment.

Task: Draft Letter to Employees
Expected Result: Have a one-page letter ready to get board approval in the XYZ board meeting

Task: Get Three Printing Quotations
Expected Result: Be ready to send print job to printer at the end of this month

Task: Select a Distribution Vendor
Expected Result: Have a vendor ready to distribute print job within four days of completion of printing

Task: Get Bids on Three Meeting Locations
Expected Result: Know 30 days in advance the exact costs involved in having our staff retreat held off-site

Before long, team members will start to negotiate times. Someone will say, "I need to have your contribution before November 15 so I can use your data to bring my part of the project together. Can you move your deadline?"

Don't accept "as soon as possible," "first quarter," or any other generality for a deadline. For a strategic plan looking out over three to five years, "first quarter" may be specific enough. But on a six-month project, "first quarter" means nothing. The "first of the first quarter" is 90 days different from the "last of the first quarter," and that's half the time allotted for the whole project.

Parties will get more involved and more committed as they negotiate deadlines. With the three headers, you can see when a task has no owner or the deadline is missing. Make your group slow down, focus, and think through their actions. Then once all of your tasks, assignments, deadlines, and expected results are in place, ask your team:

- "Are we going to pull all this off?"
- "Can we do it?"
- "Look at this in the context of other things you are doing."

Help your team to be realistic regarding what they can and will do. Push hard to convey this message: "We have this project down to these key concepts. Now it is up to you to move it forward with these specific action steps. If anyone is not committed to pulling off the plan, let's recognize that now and deal with it."

Teams invent other ways to organize. For example, on a project with many parts covering a long period, you may want to represent each person with a different colored dot. Then when your task is finished, mark an X on your dot. Construct a plan that works for you and your organization. Whatever your approach, keep it simple.

The simplest organization approach is to use your concept or project board to organize and track your action. We used this method to fix up our house following a disastrous rain storm during a roof-repair project. The work to be completed in each room became our action plan. Cost estimates were written on the various cards. Each repair was marked with an X as it was completed. This worked so well, the contractor began to use it on other projects. He said it saves one or two days working with his customers to determine what has to be done.

Organization storyboards are effective for tracking day-to-day activities in your office. The following examples cover standard activities in The McNellis Company:

Compression Planning Institute
This is the planning board for our McNellis Institutes. It shows how many people have signed up, what we have sent them, whether or not their registration fees have been received, etc. The board is hung in a place accessible to everybody who works on these activities. We can

be informed without having to ask someone else or call a meeting.

Client Status Board

The client status board is a quick reference available to everyone in the office. When I return from a trip, I look at it to see what has changed, who has been added, who has cancelled, etc. This board is a barometer of how well the business is operating in the short term. We post two months out.

LAS Assignments (Lead – Assist - Support)

This board covers facilitation and seminar assignments. Its simple matrix takes short and long-term views. Each project has an LAS team assigned. The team is comprised of a lead instructor, an assistant who helps the facilitator on site, and the support person in our headquarters who handles the details of equipment, logistics, travel, communications, supplies, materials, hotel, and food.

The LAS board covers some 200 bits of information related to scheduling, planning, and purchasing. This helps us batch materials so we can save with quantity discounts. This board is used for quick reference, and is displayed where everybody can get to it. We keep it simple and current with cards that can be moved, replaced, updated, supplemented, and thrown out.

Critical Projects

A month's projects are listed on this storyboard and assignments are made against these. Each project is given an order of priority. "Must" projects are tagged so they are sure to be finished during the month. Dots mean the projects are completed. The presentation is simple and always in front of us.

This type of board works for an organization or department that is interactive. It gives everyone knowledge of what has to be done, who is to do it, and where they stand on the month's requirements. It is reviewed at the end of the month and integrated into the next month's plan.

Business Plan

Another board covers all special projects. These backstage activities support our client work. The major thrusts: product development, sales, service, marketing, staff development, finance, technology, delivery of Institutes, client facilitation work, public relations, and communications.

Our steering team meets quarterly to review and adjust this plan and to set goals for the next quarter. The board lists projects and names of staff and outside support people who will get them done. Each person is represented by a different color dot. Half moons mark all of the active projects in the current quarter.

Each person can look at this plan and know what he or she is responsible for, what other projects are underway, which are current and which are scheduled for later.

As this illustrates, storyboards can be adapted for many jobs. They are indispensable in our shop. Maybe they could be useful to you also.

Chapter 18: Spreading The Word

The communications phase, although simple in design, is crucial to effective planning. Communications may be as simple as telling a few people about your planning session. Or, you may reach out to your entire organization and require public disclosure.

Closing down a plant or the acquisition of a new company are sensitive issues in any organization. The timing of one-on-one conversations, announcements, meetings, and news releases must be scheduled with great care. For example, union stewards should learn about a plant closing before your rank and file. If an acquisition is "material" to future earnings, simultaneous disclosure to the public is required by law.

If your communications are complicated and your audiences are numerous, you will need to break your information into specific messages that can be customized for each audience. Not every person will need to know everything. Some individuals or groups will require more details than others.

For some projects, your communications plan may be simple: "We just need to meet with our staff and brief them on what we've done." Your briefing can be in front of your storyboards, where you talk through your concepts and action plans.

On a complex issue, where many people will be affected, develop an approach that includes detailed communications as your final step in your planning. When our planning specialists facilitate two or three-day Compression Strategy Conferences, the teams devote the last hour or two to working through communications needs.

Communications should never be assigned as an afterthought.

Work through your headers in sequence until your total plan takes shape. Then rework the parts until your group is satisfied and ready to move. Here are the headers:

Step #1: Who Needs to Know
List your target groups with whom you will need to communicate. For example, consider what happens when your top seven or eight people in a business unit go away for a planning session. What do they say to their staffs back on the job Monday morning?

Maybe your group decided to put in a new receivables system. Responsibility for detailed planning and execution will be assigned to a project team, but something has to be said now. The question is, which key people need to know what was decided? Your list might include:
- Invited participants who did not attend
- Other senior management staff
- Your top four or five vendors (by name)
- Financial department managers

Your list may include four or five people, but their support could be essential to your project. Get them lined up against your plan with their noses out of joint and you are in trouble. When decisions affect large segments of your company, your entire organization needs to know, in addition to selected customers, most vendors, and maybe even community leaders. Sometimes it's all of your employees, sometimes it isn't. Think it through and focus on who needs to know.

When we were planning to relocate The McNellis Company offices, once the go-ahead decision was made, we started with this list, and it grew:

WHO NEEDS TO KNOW
- Neighbors
- Freight company
- Insurance company
- Travel agents
- Bank
- Post office
- Gas company
- Electric company
- Clients

Step #2: Specific Messages (Optional)

If yours is a complex issue, use a Specific Messages header. Print and number each message to make selection easy when you construct your communications plan. Select message numbers appropriate for each audience. Here's a sample of the basic information concerning our move:

Specific Messages

1. The McNellis Company is moving to

   _____

2. Our telephone and fax numbers are unchanged.

3. The moving date is June 1.

4. We will be conducting business at both locations from May 27 through June 4.

Plus a whole lot more messages.

Step #3: What They Need to Know

Next in your communications plan is to develop information you need to pass on. Some information will be basic and should go to everyone on your list. For example, the new location of our office was important to everyone. Other facts will be important only to certain individuals and organizations.

Once you complete your general messages, work through your "who" cards one by one and write the specific messages. The post office, for example, needs to know when to stop service at the old address and when to start at the new place. That information is for the post office. It would also apply to the telephone, gas, electric, and water companies.

Organize all of your messages and number each one so that you can write message numbers next to each "who." For example:

WHO NEEDS TO KNOW	WHAT THEY NEED TO KNOW
Gas Company	1, 2, 3, 4, 6, 8
Light Company	1, 2, 3, 4, 6, 10, 12

Step #4: Methods of Communicating

Most communications are handled through established channels: staff meetings, emails, letters, bulletin boards, etc. For simple projects, your plan will be elementary and quickly done:

"Judy, you call a Monday morning senior staff meeting for one-half hour and give them a briefing."

"Sam, you fill out a change-of-address form at the post office."

Another plan may be simple in concept but not so quickly done: "We'll do a one-page memo for all of the troops and follow up with department meetings in which the general manager will report and answer questions."

Some issues are so sensitive and important, your team will set up a task group to design a detailed plan to insure that messages get to everyone who needs to know, with precise timing and no slip-ups. Your campaign may be carried out over weeks or months and include surveys to test knowledge, understanding, and support for your project.

Step #6: Who Will Do It
The answer depends on the complexity of your issue and your plan. One person may be responsible for calling a meeting or writing a letter. Complicated and extended projects require help from communications specialists.

Step #7: Deadline
Think through when your communicating will be done and write a plan. The timing may not seem important to you (after all, you helped create the plan), but for others, your team's plan could be great news or job threatening.

The Plan is the Thing
The most important point about the Communications Phase is that your team has thought through what should be done and has a plan to carry it out. Your plan is constructed on a storyboard where it can be seen as a whole. With the grid format, conflicts, overlaps, and omissions can be caught and corrected. Responsibility is assigned and your whole team knows what results to expect.

Communications is handled at three levels in Compression Planning.

First, it may be the topic of a compression session. A team may, for example, wish to develop a plan for improving communications with the company's top five distributors.

Second, storyboards are themselves a communications vehicle. They provide all-at-onceness information for your planning group. Your boards can also be used to communicate with other groups who have a stake in your issue.

Third, the communications phase is a step in the Compression Planning System in which your team plans to inform others about your session and about actions that will follow. Be sure to ask who is functionally important and/or politically wise to be sure you are in contact with.

Chapter 19: Lessons We Have Learned

At the beginning of every project, you should ask yourself and your client: "What do we want to achieve?" We could do a perfect job solving the problem in four months, or we could do a 60 percent job in two days. What's required? Perfection or 60 percent?"

Most of the time the answer will be: "Sixty percent in two days. We'll go for another 60 percent in the next cut!"

When You Are Asked to Lead

If you are asked to facilitate a Compression Planning session and you sense your client isn't committed to making something happen, walk away. If he is committed, work with him to design a focused session.

TO IDENTIFY THE SIX MAJOR CAUSES OF THE PROBLEM AND DEVELOP GAME PLANS FOR RESOLVING THEM

With a good design in hand, you can recruit participants who will commit to developing a plan to resolve the issue or issues.

Even with outstanding design and commitment from your client, not every Compression Planning session will succeed. However, your odds for a positive outcome are in your favor. Out of 10 sessions you design and lead, eight will far surpass anything you've ever done before. Your ninth will be so-so. From your tenth, you will learn a lot. Eight out of 10. Not bad odds.

I have had participants come to groups committed to sabotaging the effort. I remember three in detail. Two saboteurs did not succeed. The third ended up as spokesperson for the new game plan, after admitting to the group what his intention had been. "As I have come to understand the issue," he said, "I can see there are no options. We must succeed together or go down together. I'm ready to join the team and work for success."

Frustration at the Top

The following Compression Planning session didn't fly. They failed to accomplish their design or purpose, but I learned from them. The facts have been altered so nobody, with the possible exception of the clients, will recognize the organizations. The first group, from a Fortune 100 corporation, was comprised of the chairman/CEO, president, four operating vice-presidents, and six other senior managers. Their purpose was to develop a breakthrough idea with more profit potential than the rest of the corporation combined in the first 18 months.

After the division head (who hired me) and I designed the session, he decided to bring in another consultant to act as co-facilitator and content specialist. I was to handle process. The combination did not work. We were too polite to step on the other's toes. Each wanted to make the other look good.

Most threatening of all was the senior officer who forced himself on the team. His total effect was to shoot down every idea. Nobody was willing (or strong enough) to neutralize him. The outcome was predictable. The session failed. Everybody just wanted to leave – which they did – without making any decisions.

I wanted to crawl away and hide because I wanted to be a successful facilitator. I wanted those people to think I was the greatest facilitator who ever walked or wiggled. Instead, I believed they thought I was some schlock. Ten months later, when I ran into the person who had hired me, I asked, "Are you still speaking to me?" "You shouldn't feel that way," he replied. "I know you thought that session was a disaster, but let me tell you what happened as a result."

"First, we found out we can't do what we tried to do at that level in the organization. We stopped trying. Second, some division people in the session asked us to help them with other projects. And that is working well."

 He saw benefits I was in no position to see. If I hadn't run into him in the Atlanta airport, I would have carried the sense of failure maybe forever. As it was, I learned these valuable lessons:

1. Never work as co-facilitator with some one you don't know and whose style is different from your own. One or the other can facilitate the group but not both of you.

2. Individual participants, and sometimes your entire group, can be laboring over other issues so large your group is powerless to confront the real purpose of your session.

3. Timing can be wrong.

4. The "gorilla who sleeps anywhere he wants to" can take control and there is nothing the facilitator can do to stop him.

5. Groups often learn from "failed"

sessions.

6. As the neutral facilitator, you cannot take responsibility for the "givens" of your client and his team or the eventual outcome of the project.

Lesson six above should be taken as a caution by new facilitators. After you have facilitated Compression Planning sessions for your own issues for a while, you will be asked to do it for others. Don't be so quick to agree. Study the givens, and insofar as you are able, make sure your session is not doomed to failure.

Two Merged Organizations
The second example involved two boards of directors who had voted to merge their organizations and were trying to sort out the functions. It was obvious they were not going to support two purchasing groups, two management information functions, two human resources departments, and so on. Even though the organizations had merged on paper, it was soon apparent they had not merged in spirit. Two departments that had to consolidate for the merger to succeed were mixing like water and oil. Finally, they were told, "Get together and work it out!" Our team was hired to design and facilitate a Compression Planning session that would pull off the miracle.

The night before we were to convene, some of the parties met with their attorneys to decide whether or not they would even attend the session. Wisdom, curiosity, or more likely, battle tactics prevailed and they showed up. As an opening wedge, I asked everyone to draw a picture of how he or she perceived the relationship between the organizations. They turned in sketches of people shooting arrows and plunging knives into others' backs.

Later, trying to force confrontation of the real issue, I told them, "For the next 40 minutes, I want each of you to assume the role of your counterpart at your biggest competitor." Each person was given the name tag of his or her competitive equivalent.

"Here is the situation. You are the competitor meeting two miles up the road trying to figure out how to bury this merged group. What questions are you asking about your big new competitor?" We printed all of their questions on cards and pinned them on a storyboard:

- How long will they screw around trying to get going?
- How can we capitalize on their infighting?
- What can we do to make sure they keep fighting each other?
- How can we hire their best people while they slug it out?

As each new question was added to the board, the group felt the real issue starting to gnaw at them. The pain showed in their faces, posture, and through the growing silence. They understood, many for the first time, that while they had come to the session to rearrange the deck chairs, their Titanic was plunging to the ocean floor. They were going down together unless they mounted a rescue operation at once.

This was the most complex, difficult, and emotionally exhausting session I had ever facilitated. Months later, I heard our client had resigned to become president of another medical center. My hopes sank with the news.

We didn't hear any more for two years. Then to our amazement and great delight, we received an invitation to a reunion of the planning team to be held at the time of an open house of their new facility. Enclosed with the invitation were drawings made during the strategy conference to show how they envisioned the new organization. They had managed to overcome their fear, panic, and anger. They were making the merger work, but not without a lot of struggle and personal commitment.

The lessons I learned from this experience:

- The facilitator cannot be the leader. The leader has to lead. Every so often, a facilitator will tell us of his frustration with the outcome of a compression session. I ask, "Is this a Compression Planning issue or a leadership issue?" You must be clear on who owns the issue and who is responsible for doing something about it.
- The team has to get behind the leader.
- Your instant low from a session may not be any more valid than your instant high. What you need to ask is, "Did something of long-term significance result?"

One of the First Hard Lessons

When I first started as a professional facilitator, I was brought in to help with a session for the president of an organization. All of my directions came from her executive director, who assigned the project to a staff person, who hired a consultant, who hired me. I was five steps removed from the real client.

The lesson I learned was work with the real leader or with a team including the leader. I wasn't even close to the leader. Data we were given were not valid.

Chapter 20: Bear Traps And Final Thoughts

Sometime, after you have begun to facilitate Compression Planning sessions, you will be asked to "do one of those storyboard things for me." The attention will feel great. Like most of us who have found something that works, you will be eager to help. But watch out. There could be a bear trap hidden there somewhere.

Ask lots of questions. Design thoroughly. Don't let your good intentions plunge you into a situation where failure is guaranteed.

One hidden agenda often encountered is where someone wants you to bring her group around to a predetermined conclusion on an issue. Her objective, often unstated, strives to "get people on board." In my opinion, this is unethical, if not dishonest. If you try to manipulate a group to a predetermined position, they will blame your process. Why not? It's easier (and safer!) than blaming the boss.

A client may say up front, "Here's a plan I have in mind; however, I'm open to other approaches. I'll hold back my plan and not steer the participants." The risk is worth taking when you can have some confidence your client is ready to consider other possibilities.

A legitimate team can be asked to respond to a plan it feels free to adjust and change. But in my experience, people will not get on board with something already invented, unless the leader is a skilled manipulator. Most are not that skilled. Team members can tell whether or not the dialogue is honest. They sense what is going on and refuse to risk their egos and future careers in such a game.

Support Where You Least Expect It

We were engaged by the executive officer of a professional society to facilitate a compression session in which the president was a participant. I click with most people, but not this man. He isn't on my Christmas card list. He challenged me on everything. I felt no chemistry between us. Yet, two days later he called and asked us to do a similar session for his staff.

Just because somebody seems as though he is not with you doesn't mean he is not. On the other hand, somebody who looks committed 100 percent may be off in fog land. In one audience to whom I spoke, a woman in the front row sat on her feet and crocheted the whole time. She took no notes and appeared not to listen. Weeks later, she telephoned to tell me the amazing things she was doing with Compression Planning.

One of my favorite axioms:

> *"Leaders plan and lead
> from their plan."*

Who's In Charge Anyway?

The Compression Planning System helps leaders do better planning, and it gives them documentation from which to lead. A client "hires" a facilitator, but it is the client's responsibility – not the facilitator's – to lead and manage.

You see high implementation coming out of Compression Planning sessions most of the time because the participants write the plan. I hire you to go off and write a plan and come back and say, "You ought to do this." But I have no ownership in the plan. Where's my investment, my blood, sweat, toil, and tears? On the other hand, if you facilitate, and I collaborate in a team effort to develop a plan…team members commit to each other…the odds of successful implementation increase.

That's how it works, most of the time. Yet people at the end of some sessions will say, "Well now, that was the easy part, the tough part lays ahead of us. We must make sure we pull it off."

My response: "If you came here, went through these hours of work, and at this point you are not committed to your plan, this was just an exercise in the woods."

I despise the word "exercise" when it refers to serious work. Business people shouldn't engage in intellectual exercise. We are not paid to exercise. We are paid to plan and execute a plan. To me, the term "exercise" has the connotation nothing will come of it, that planning is meaningless.

Compression Planning is not intended to be play, although it's normally enjoyable. It moves an issue from wherever it is (many times from "talking") into focused action people commit to doing.

Aligning Your Forces

It's unrealistic to expect every project will go just the way it was planned. Many adjustments were made during Voyager's journey to Neptune, but the accuracy of its travel over 12 years is the equivalent of shooting a dart from New York and hitting a postage stamp in San Francisco. Space journeys to the moon were in adjustment mode 98 percent of the time, according to Charles Garfield in Peak Performers.

Set your sights and be prepared for adjustments.

People plan in compression mode expecting to make decisions and get things done. They may go all the way through a session and conclude: "We can't do it." That's good planning, to discover you can't do something. To say, "We are going to do it" when everybody knows you are not going to do it, is being a charlatan. It's dishonest!

Your Plate Should Not Be Overloaded

I remember reading, "If you work on more than two or three projects, you work on nothing." That's wisdom. Your ideal would be for a dedicated team to plan in a compression mode and then follow through full time. It's an ideal, although it seldom happens.

One project I facilitated involved two people who invited 12 others to join them in a planning session. One or two participants came away with assignments, but the two clients were responsible for delivery on their plan.

Prime-Time Planning

In a perfect world, every group, before they go into an off-site Compression Planning session, would get away and relax for two days so they could come in "de-cluttered." This never happens. Fresh, open people working at compression pace can accomplish a phenomenal amount. But it takes energy.

Many clients start out saying, "Can we do this over a weekend?" In big corporations, this is not much of an issue any more. They used to say, "You know, we can't take our people out of the day-to-day business. Why don't we start on a Friday night and work until midnight and go all day Saturday?" I would ask, "What's your normal physical state on a Friday evening?" Their response: "What do you mean?"

Then I would ask, "Aren't you tired?" Their response: "Exhausted." Finally, I would ask, "Are you telling me you want to go exhausted into what could be your most critical thinking session this year?" Tell me that makes sense.

Big "P," little "E"

Many years ago, I met a Japanese woman. It was before Americans were telling each other how the Japanese do things. She was a pharmacist in a hospital, and I said, "Will you describe for me the difference between Japanese and American management?"

She walked over to a flipchart and drew two sketches: a large circle with a "P" in it, and a small circle with an "E" in it. The other sketch showed the P in a small circle and the E in a large circle.

"These are the Japanese," she explained, pointing to the sketch with the P in the large circle. "We plan for a long time. When we achieve consensus, we are ready to move fast and not waste resources."

"You Americans over here [she pointed] expend little effort planning before you move to execution. As a result, you do a lot of your planning with trial and error on your production floor."

A lot of people start into implementation before they plan, and then they must stop, go back, and re-do. I heard of a situation in which an organization was moving into a building while the managers were still trying to figure out where the walls should go. Logic tells me this is not the most efficient way to work. In Compression Planning, we advise:

 Think ahead, plan it, and then move.

In this book we provided you with tools, methods and leadership principles to help you plan. These ideas can be adapted to your team's leadership approach to meet your unique needs.

Now It's Up to You

It is said when a student is ready, the teacher appears. The source of this wisdom is lost to me, yet my experience confirms its truth. We wrote this book for those ready to help themselves and others work be more effective in collaborative thinking, planning, and doing. Our greatest reward will be if, after reading our book, you are better equipped to lead teams who want to make a difference. Just too many important things need to get done not to give it a try. When you use The McNellis Compression Planning System, you will make a difference. You will grow and other people will grow with you.

About the Author: Jerry McNellis

Jerry McNellis has been sharing the powerful process of Compression Planning with key decision makers all across the country for over thirty years.

Jerry's specialty is helping organizations cut through the clutter to laser in on a strategic target incredibly quickly and effectively.

Before launching the McNellis Compression Planning Institute, Jerry applied his insights and creative thinking as the Director of Chambers of Commerce in both Minnesota and Pennsylvania.

The foundation of Jerry's creative thinking really started as a child when he experienced a challenge that defined the rest of his life in the most positive way.

He contracted polio. In fact, Jerry spent at least five years of his childhood confined to a hospital.

Forced by a wayward virus to look inward for his adventures, Jerry developed an unshakable resilience and curiosity about life. His parents taught him there were simply no limits to what he could accomplish.

This experience became a powerful springboard for his life. Eventually, Jerry was mentored by one of the most creative minds of modern times, the creator of "displayed thinking®" for Disney, Mike Vance. The innovative result? Compression Planning was born.

His warm, down-to-earth approach combines a transformational process for strategic thinking and decision making into a surprisingly easy-to- understand process

Some of Jerry's clients include The Watson Institute, the Cleveland Clinic, General Mills, Hilton Hotels, the Department of Energy, Habitat for Humanity, Humana, Matthews International, and Thought Form Design, as well as numerous higher educational institutions.

And what they have all discovered is, Compression Planning is critical for resolving complex issues in record time. In fact Jerry's clients use Compression Planning with their clients, such as McDonald's, Steelcase, Carnegie Museums, Nike, and American Express.

The proven results speak for themselves: actionable plans 30-75% FASTER, massive savings to your bottom line, and employees who are frequently 100% vested in the outcome.

When he isn't leading Compression Planning Workshops, Jerry loves spending time with his wife and best friend Phyllis and their family. Jerry admits to being a rabid C-SPAN fan, and loves kicking back in his recliner with a good book.

To explore how Jerry McNellis and his team can equip individuals or teams within your company or organization to tackle your critical issues by using Compression Planning, contact him at 1-800-569-6015 or email jerry@compressionplanning.com.

For more resources on the McNellis Accelerated Planning Systems, please visit the following websites:

1. www.compressionplanning.com

2. www.mycpcommunity.com

3. www.executivedecisionmakingsystems.com

4. www.storyboardtools.com

To learn more about the McNellis Company services and products...

Visit the following Web sites:

www.compressionplanning.com
www.mycpcommunity.com
www.exeutivedecisionmakingsystems.com (you'll find Jerry's blog for senior leaders here)

For more information about the McNellis Compression Planning Advantage, including the Compression Planning Institute, contact Institute Concierge Stephanie McNellis at 800-569-6015 or at Stephanie@compressionplanning.com.

If you are interested in learning more about having McNellis professional facilitators design and lead a Compression Planning session for your key people on a "pivotal issue," "strategic questions," or a "huge opportunity," please contact Pat@compressionplanning.com.

If you would like to inquire about having the McNellis team conduct Compression Planning training for your business or organization at your desired location, please contact Dianne@compressionplanning.com.

If you'd like to talk with Jerry McNellis, send him an e-mail at jerry@compressionplanning.com or call 724-746-1220.

We highly recommend **Storyboard Tools** as your source for storyboard supplies. We buy and rent from them and they are our backstage provider, so you can rest assured that they are first class and dependable.

For more information on products, contact:
Storyboard Tools - www.storyboardtools.com
Kim McDemus - kim@storyboardtools.com
1445 Washington Road, Suite 400
Washington, PA 15301
Phone: 724-229-0954 or Fax: 724-229-3052

McNellis & Associates
715 15th Avenue
Beaver Falls, PA 15010
724-847-2120
800-569-6015

Made in the USA
Las Vegas, NV
14 September 2021